SARAH BERNHARDT

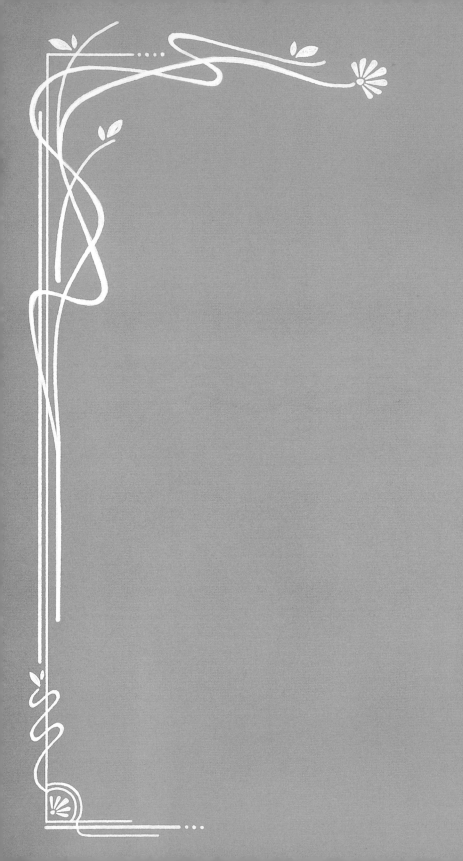

SARAH BERNHARDT

THE DIVINE AND DAZZLING LIFE
OF THE WORLD'S FIRST SUPERSTAR

CATHERINE REEF

CLARION BOOKS
HOUGHTON MIFFLIN HARCOURT
BOSTON   NEW YORK

CLARION BOOKS
3 Park Avenue
New York, New York 10016

Clarion Books is an imprint of
Houghton Mifflin Harcourt Publishing Company.

hmhbooks.com

The text was set in ITC Legacy Serif.
Hand-lettering and illustrations by Ellen Duda.
Book design by Ellen Duda.

Library of Congress Cataloging-in-Publication Data
Names: Reef, Catherine, author.
Title: Sarah Bernhardt / Catherine Reef.
Description: Boston : Clarion Books/Houghton Mifflin Harcourt, [2020]
Includes bibliographical references. | Audience: Ages: 12+. | Audience: Grades: 7-8.
Summary: "A tantalizing biography for teens on Sarah Bernhardt, the first international
celebrity and one of the greatest actors of all time, who lived a highly unconventional,
utterly fascinating life. Illustrated with more than sixty-five photos of Bernhardt
on stage, in film, and in real life"— Provided by publisher.
Identifiers: LCCN 2019017244 | ISBN 9781328557506 (hardcover)
Subjects: LCSH: Bernhardt, Sarah, 1844-1923—Juvenile literature.
Actresses—France—Biography--Juvenile literature.
Classification: LCC PN2638.B5 R44 2020 | DDC 792.02/8092 [B]–dc23
LC record available at https://lccn.loc.gov/2019017244

Manufactured in China
SCP 10 9 8 7 6 5 4 3 2 1
4500796101

FOR CHANTAL TOUZET-BUSH

THE NINETEENTH CENTURY WILL BE CALLED
THE CENTURY OF SARAH BERNHARDT.

—JEAN RAMEAU, journalist

CONTENTS

FACE-TO-FACE

There are five kinds of actresses: bad actresses,
fair actresses, good actresses, great actresses—
and then there is Sarah Bernhardt.
—widely attributed to Mark Twain, writer

Who was this odd young woman? Félix Duquesnel, the new manager of Paris's Odéon Theater, had never seen anyone like her. She had paraded into his study as if the world were watching. Behind her trailed a nursemaid holding a plump, pink boy about eighteen months old. Duquesnel guessed that the child was the young woman's son.

Her name was Sarah Bernhardt, and she was twenty-one. Was she tall? No, that was an illusion. She was petite, standing just over five feet in height. She only appeared tall because she carried herself with such confidence. Her eyes—were they blue? It was hard to tell. At times they flashed gold or green in the midday sunlight that filtered through the blinds. And how strangely she was dressed! On her frizzy, reddish-blond hair was perched a straw hat with bells hanging from its brim. She had tied a feathered fan at her slender waist, and she wore a Chinese high-collared blouse with shiny embroidery. Duquesnel's maid thought she must have come from the other side of the world.

The manager was bewitched. "She was not pretty," he thought, but she possessed some other, more compelling quality for which he had no name. "I found myself face-to-face with a marvelously gifted creature, intelligent, nearly a genius," he sensed, someone "of great energy."

Bernhardt plays the leading female role in Jean Racine's classical drama *Phèdre*.

Her voice, he said, was "pure as crystal. Sweet as heavenly music, it went straight to one's heart."

It was June 1866, and Bernhardt was asking for a job. Her timing could not have been better, because Duquesnel was looking for new actors to breathe life into the plays presented at the Odéon. Secretly, he hoped to discover a star. There were reasons to think that Bernhardt was a poor choice for what he had in mind, however. She had trained as an actor and even worked as one, but her temper had earned her a reputation for trouble. And reviews of her acting were so-so at best. Still, Duquesnel saw potential in her. With the right direction, he believed, this Sarah Bernhardt could go far.

And so she did. She became a bigger star than Félix Duquesnel or anyone else could have imagined. For decades in the nineteenth and twentieth centuries, she ruled the theater world in Paris and had countless fans throughout the world. She entertained royalty in palaces and ordinary folk in tents. Crowds everywhere showered her with flowers.

A true original, Bernhardt filled her home with palm trees, statues, bearskin rugs, curios from around the world, and a menagerie of exotic pets. She dressed to please herself in lace, furs, and eccentric hats. Others copied her style, but she never imitated anyone.

The public knew many different Sarahs. There was Sarah in costume, wearing jeweled headdresses, veils and wigs, silks and brocades. Audiences saw her as a queen of Egypt or Byzantium, as prince of Denmark or Joan of Arc. They watched her die onstage thousands of times in all kinds of ways: from poison, stabbing, a snakebite, or jumping off a roof. "I have touched real death in my different deaths," Bernhardt wrote. "My face has been bloodless, my heart has almost stopped beating, my lungs have stopped breathing."

There was Sarah the world traveler, shooting a gun in Brazil, meeting the great Houdini in Boston, or perching at the edge of Niagara Falls.

Sarah Bernhardt was famous for her onstage deaths. She observed the dying and dead in hospitals and morgues to make her death scenes seem realistic.

Then there was Sarah the patriot. Devoted to her beloved France, she supported her country in times of war, nursing wounded soldiers or performing for troops at the front lines.

The public knew Sarah the mother, and later Sarah the grandmother. Briefly, they knew Sarah the wife. They knew Sarah the sculptor, dressed in trousers and holding a chisel, and Sarah the author of popular books. They had seen pictures of her, too many to count: Sarah sleeping in a coffin or wearing a stuffed bat on her head; Sarah floating in a hot-air balloon; Sarah playing tennis or riding a horse.

Golden-voiced Sarah. Divine Sarah.

No one ever forgot seeing Bernhardt act. She walked onstage with a smile, as if thanking the audience for coming. Briefly she was herself; then she transformed into her character almost by magic. People remarked again and again that they fell under a spell. They forgot

A hat topped with a stuffed bat was one of the most eccentric items in Bernhardt's wardrobe.

they were watching Sarah Bernhardt and believed they were seeing Cleopatra, Prince Hamlet, the queen of Spain, or whatever character she was portraying. She spoke her lines in that clear, musical voice, now uttering strings of words quickly, now barely managing to whisper a syllable. She used her whole body to communicate, giving meaning to every tilt of her head and movement of her hands. Onstage, she loved;

she hoped; she was betrayed; she suffered. At an intensely dramatic moment, she might extend an arm and hold it in the air for a second, or two, or three. Audiences cried with her; they laughed, they cheered, and they adored her.

Creating the illusion took hours of practice, because Bernhardt had set herself a lofty goal. As she explained, "What I am trying to show you is human nature as it has shown itself to me."

ONE

WHAT CAN BE
DONE WITH SARAH?

Meek,
Chic,
Very
Merry!
You are just the huckleberry
Of our dreams . . .
—Anonymous, "An Ode to Sara"

Sarah Bernhardt claimed that when she was three years old, she fell out of her highchair and into a burning hearth. Acting fast, her nurse snatched her from the fire and plunged her into a pail of fresh milk. *Dieu merci!* The nurse, an old farm woman, treated Sarah's burns in the only way she knew, by spreading butter on them. She also sent for the little girl's mother.

Soon, there she was: golden-haired, showy, and looking like a saint to Sarah's eyes. Once she was sure that her daughter would be fine, Sarah's mother left the farm in northern France where the aging couple—the nurse and her husband—looked after the child for a fee.

Sarah's beautiful mother! Her name was Judith, but she went by Youle, or sometimes Julie. She used the last name Van Hard, but the family name was closer to Bernard or Bernardt. Sarah would spell it

Sarah Bernhardt as the Empress Théodora
in Sardou's *Théodora*

Sarah Bernhardt's first home was a Brittany farmhouse with
a kitchen hearth much like this one.

Bernhardt. Sarah's mother had been born into a Jewish family in the
Netherlands. She and her sister Rosine left home as young teenagers.
They made their way to Switzerland, London, and finally Le Havre,
on France's northern coast. Little is known about Youle's early life,
but records show that in Le Havre she gave birth to twin girls, who
soon died.

The sisters moved on to Paris, where Youle found work as a
seamstress. At sixteen she had another baby, a girl who lived. Sarah
Bernhardt said that she was born on October 22, 1844, and maybe she
was. A fire destroyed her birth certificate, so she can only be taken at
her word.

In Paris, Youle and Rosine slipped into the *demimonde*. This was a level of society that thrived apart from "respectable" city life. Devoted to creativity and erotic pleasure, the demimonde had no physical boundaries; it was defined by its live-and-let-live approach to life. Proper ladies never ventured into the demimonde, although their husbands might seek its delights. Artists, writers, and performers frequented its dance halls. Gay men and lesbians found acceptance there. The demimonde was the world of the courtesans. These women earned a good living by offering companionship and sex to men who paid them handsomely. This was the life that Youle and Rosine found. Another sister, Henriette, also lived in France, but she had married a businessman and lived a conventional life.

Men commonly visited sex workers in the cities of nineteenth-century France. Often, a young man went to a house of prostitution for the first time with his father. This practice was considered part of a youth's education, a way of teaching him about sex and female bodies. It was thought important for boys to acquire this knowledge, whereas girls—whose virginity had to be protected—were kept ignorant.

Just as a rigid class system divided society, there were levels of prestige among sex workers. At the bottom were streetwalkers. These poor, desperate women solicited customers from sidewalks and doorways. Above them were women employed in houses of prostitution. They lived and worked under the supervision of a madam, a woman with years of experience in the sex trade and an aptitude for business. Courtesans were at the peak of their profession. They catered to men who were wealthy, connected to royalty, or powerful in the sphere of politics, finance, or the arts. A visit to an ordinary prostitute was kept discreet, but a courtesan was to be shown off and showered with money and costly gifts. She was a status symbol, proof that a man belonged to the privileged class.

A courtesan offered more than sex. Customers paid lavishly to bask in her charm, escort her to the theater, and have her as a traveling companion. Some evenings, they gathered in her salon to engage in clever conversation and tell risqué stories. The money she earned allowed a courtesan to live independently in gracious surroundings and wear expensive clothes. "Honest work would never have brought me the luxury I craved," said one courtesan. "I wanted to know the refinements and pleasures of artistic taste, the joy of living in elegant and cultivated society." Her life was not very different from that of her clients' aristocratic wives, but she would never have been accepted as their equal.

Courtesans were known for their beauty, intelligence, and nonconformist ways. They spurned marriage or respectable work in favor of a life that offered money and freedom. Many courtesans, among them Youle Van Hard, changed their names. Turning their backs on the past, they reinvented themselves. Some courtesans even became celebrities. These were women like Cora Pearl, whose real name was Emma Crouch. Pearl loved horses and owned as many as sixty. She maintained two homes, a sumptuous Paris apartment and a grand chateau in the Loire valley. Another famous courtesan, Liane de Pougy (born Anne Marie Chassaigne), bragged to the press about the value of her jewels. She owned a diamond-and-ruby serpent worth nine hundred thousand francs, she said, a pearl collar worth one hundred thirty thousand francs, and another pearl necklace valued at seventy-five thousand francs. Most courtesans, including Van Hard, never achieved this level of wealth and fame, but they did live quite comfortably.

By the time Sarah was five, she and her nurse were dwelling in a small, nearly windowless apartment in Paris. The nurse's husband had died, and she had married again. Her new spouse was the building's *concierge,* or superintendent. For Sarah, life felt "black, black!" In years to come, she would grow to love the beauty and cheery bustle of Paris, but not yet. She was homesick for the landscape she knew, the green hills and rocky coast of Brittany, in northern France. Mostly she missed her mother, whom she rarely saw. Youle Van Hard still paid the nurse to take care of Sarah. She, too, lived in Paris, but Sarah never saw her.

Finally, one day something wondrous happened. A carriage pulled into the building's courtyard, and a stylish lady stepped out. She was someone Sarah knew: Aunt Rosine! The little girl ran to her aunt and wrapped her thin arms around her. Rosine gave money to the nurse.

Young Sarah hungered for her mother's love and approval.

Then, with her errand completed, she tried to pry Sarah's hands from her lacy sleeves, but the child could not be budged. Rosine promised to return for her the next day, and Sarah relaxed her grip. Seconds later, though, as she watched her aunt climb into the carriage, she worried. What if Rosine was lying? What if she was telling the truth but forgot to come back?

Desperate to stop her aunt from leaving, Sarah threw herself to the pavement in front of the carriage. She fell hard, blacking out and possibly breaking her arm. At least, that's the tale she told when she wrote her memoirs as an adult. Another time she said that she jumped from a window onto the paving stones. Either way, it was a dramatic story, but when Sarah Bernhardt spoke about the past, it was hard to know whether all she said was true. She once told a journalist that her mother had fourteen children, including two sets of twins, and that she was child number eleven. Why stick to plain facts when imagined scenes could be more fantastic, touching, or tragic? Bernhardt always left her audience entertained.

However it happened, Sarah was hurt badly enough to be removed from the nurse's care and taken to live in her mother's Paris flat. The next thing she remembered was waking up "in a beautiful, wide bed which smelt very nice," with a worried Youle Van Hard at her side. Sarah's mother loved her . . . didn't she?

Two years passed; for Sarah, they were years of boredom, when she played alone with her dolls under a servant's watchful eye. Her mother promised to spend time with her, but she was always too busy. Eventually it dawned on Van Hard that Sarah, age seven, could not read, write, or do simple arithmetic. She had yet to start practicing the refined skills that all young ladies mastered, such as drawing and embroidery. Maybe it was time for her to go away to school. Besides, Van Hard was pregnant again. Two youngsters were more than she wanted to handle—especially when one had such a wild, dramatic streak. She enrolled Sarah in a fashionable girls' boarding school in the suburb of Anteuil.

Throughout Europe and America in the nineteenth century, very few paths in life were open to women. Education prepared girls to be upstanding wives—modest, refined mates who adorned a man's home and hearth—and charming hostesses. Most girls aspired to marry well; that is, they hoped to wed a kind, morally upright man with an ample income and a secure place in society. It was common knowledge, though, that a suitor wanted more than a woman who could sing pretty airs and sew a fine seam. She had to come from a good family, which meant that the daughter of an unmarried courtesan would never be welcomed into the upper or middle class. At best she might find happiness with a solid, steady laborer. If unmarried, a girl like Sarah could find a job in a shop or earn her living with a sewing needle.

Luckily for Sarah, she liked school. She made friends, and the schoolmistress treated her kindly. The pupils sang rounds and raised flowers in the school's garden. Once a week, they enjoyed a visit from actors with the Comédie-Française, the famed national theater of France, who recited poetry for them. Each time, Sarah was enthralled. In the evening, she would sit on her dormitory bed and read loudly from great French tragedies. The other girls laughed, as they were bound to do, drawing embarrassed anger from Sarah. "I would then rush about to the right and the left, giving them kicks and blows," Bernhardt recalled.

When the girls staged a play of their own, Sarah was cast as the fairy queen. She practiced her part until she knew it backward and forward, and when the curtain went up, the show began well. The girls remembered their lines and moved about the stage just as they had done in rehearsals. Then the second scene started, and Sarah noticed three latecomers joining the audience. She recognized her mother, Aunt Rosine, and the duc de Morny, one of the women's male friends.

In that moment, she panicked, and everything she had practiced went right out of her head. All she could think of were the many eyes watching her, and the keen ears listening for her to make a mistake. Gripped by stage fright and nearly blinded by tears, Sarah ran from the stage and threw herself on her bed.

Youle Van Hard followed her daughter to the dormitory and stood above her, scolding. "And to think that this is a child of mine!" Sarah's heart was breaking. After her mother left, she cried so much that she made herself ill and spent four days in the infirmary. She wrestled with a question that she would still be asking in years to come: "Why had my mother been so cruel, so cold to her daughter?"

Occasionally someone else visited Sarah at school: her father. At one time, he and Van Hard were romantically involved. They no longer had any kind of relationship, and he didn't play much of a role in his child's upbringing. Still, he helped support Sarah, and he was known to her, although today his name is a mystery. It has been said that he was a naval officer, the son of a wealthy family in Le Havre. Or maybe he was a lawyer who had been studying at the University of Paris when Sarah was conceived. Whoever he was, Sarah's father was paying for her schooling. And when she was nine, he decided that she needed instruction in religion—in his religion, the Roman Catholic faith. He arranged for her to enter Notre-Dame du Grandchamp, a convent school in another suburb, Versailles.

No one told Sarah, though. She learned that she was to leave her much-loved school on the day Aunt Rosine showed up to take her away. Sarah reacted by throwing the biggest temper tantrum of her life. For two hours, her blue eyes flashed with fury. She yelled, rolled on the floor, and cursed the adults in her life. She rushed outside and threatened to jump into a muddy pond. "The idea that I was to be ordered about, without any regard to my own wishes or inclinations, put me into an indescribable rage," Bernhardt wrote. Rosine at last brought

Sarah away, not to the convent but to her own Paris apartment. There she called in a doctor to examine the exhausted child. He prescribed several weeks of rest, so Sarah went to stay with proper Aunt Henriette and her husband, Félix Faure.

Her uncle was kind, but Sarah hated her strict, unsmiling aunt. Aunt Henriette chided Sarah for her wildness, yet she conveniently failed to see that her own perfect children egged their cousin on. If they bet Sarah that she could not jump across a ditch, Sarah had to accept the challenge—even though she knew Aunt Henriette would punish her for soiling her dress.

None too soon, the day came for ten-year-old Sarah to enter the convent school. Wearing a new uniform, she set off in a carriage with her mother and father together, as they almost never were. Soon she stood before the heavy double doors of the convent. It was a solid, silent brick building that looked to Sarah like a prison. She had heard adults say that she was impossible to manage. Aunt Henriette foresaw that she would come to a bad end. Now she trembled, fearing that she was about to be locked up forever.

The doors opened, Sarah and her parents stepped inside, and Sarah discovered that her new school was not the prison she had feared. Waiting beyond the doorway was "the sweetest and merriest face imaginable," Bernhardt recalled. It belonged to Mother Sainte Sophie, the nun who oversaw Notre-Dame du Grandchamp. Sarah, a little girl desperate to be loved, flung herself into the mother superior's embrace. The kindly nun showed the newcomers around the convent school. Sarah saw the dining hall where she would eat her meals and the dormitory where she would sleep. Outdoors, Mother Sainte Sophie pointed out the plot of ground where each girl raised her own garden. Already Sarah thought about the seeds she wanted to plant.

Here was a place where she could thrive! This did not mean, though, that she was a perfect student. She earned good grades in

Though forbidding on the outside, Notre-Dame du Grandchamp,
the convent school at Versailles, was a welcoming place.

geography and did well in art classes, but in other subjects she turned in just enough work to get by. Her misbehavior led to frequent scoldings and gained her a reputation. "I became a personality," Bernhardt stated, "and that sufficed for my childish pride." Sarah was the girl who played tricks on the nuns during lessons, who mimicked the bishop for laughs. She was the one who collected small pets: lizards, crickets, and spiders. When one of her lizards died, she held a funeral for it. Some twenty girls marched in a procession, chanting a Latin prayer.

News came that the archbishop of Paris was to visit the school. To honor him, the nuns helped the girls put on a play. It told the story of Tobias, a man living in Old Testament times. With help from the Angel Raphael, Tobias restores sight to his blind father. Sarah hoped more than anything that she would be given a role. She told herself that stage fright was a thing of the past, that she had outgrown her childish fear. Then she watched as all the parts went to other students, to girls like her pretty, popular friend, Sophie Croizette. Sarah was crushed, but she was also resourceful. On the day of the performance, when the girl playing the Angel Raphael was too terror-stricken to go on, Sarah came forward. She knew all the lines, stepped into the role, and played the part without feeling afraid. She considered this her first success as an actor.

Religion was basic to convent-school life. Sarah, who had had no religious upbringing and whose mother had been raised Jewish, learned Catholic teachings. She found peace in the solemn ritual of the Catholic Mass and felt that she had found a new home in the church. She watched the nuns go about their quiet, orderly lives, praying, eating their meals, and performing humble duties at certain hours each day. Sarah imagined herself taking religious vows and spending her life behind the convent's walls, serving God with the sisters she had grown to love.

She received the church's sacraments, beginning with baptism. As the sisters explained, a priest would wash sin from her soul with a small amount of water and welcome her into the Catholic faith. Children born into Catholic homes are almost always baptized as infants, but people can be baptized at any age. Sarah's baptism took place on May 21, 1856, when she was eleven. Joining her were two strangers who did not study at the convent: her half sister Jeanne, the child born while Sarah was away at her first school, and another, younger half sister, Régine. Youle Van Hard had arranged for all three of her children to be baptized together.

Also present were Sarah's aunts, uncle, and three men who had agreed to be the girls' godfathers. Sarah's was named Régis Lavolie. He possibly was a friend of her father's, as she was told. Or he may have been one of the male companions who paid for Youle's favors. He was a gruff man whom Sarah disliked. Not there was her father, though Sarah had long imagined his pride as he watched her join his church.

Days before the baptism, Van Hard had come to the school and given Sarah the terrible news that her father had died. Sarah cried as never before for the father she had barely known. As always, her fragile health was no match for her violent emotions. A week later, after receiving the sacrament of confirmation, she fell ill again. This time she came down with pneumonia.

Hoping that pure mountain air would heal Sarah's lungs, Van Hard took her daughters for a long holiday in the Pyrenees, the mountain range separating France and Spain. The vacation gave Sarah time to get to know her half sisters. Four-year-old Jeanne, quiet and well-behaved, was their mother's pet. Van Hard often cuddled her and kissed her feet. Régine, at two, was a spunky, rebellious child, much like Sarah. Sarah understood this little girl whom their mother pushed away and formed a close, protective bond with her.

Day by day, Sarah felt her health returning. She took solitary hikes past peasants' farms, through low woods, and on the slippery turf of steep meadows. Neighboring hills looked like clusters of blue or violet clouds; beyond them rose taller, snow-covered peaks. Sarah befriended the alpine goats that grazed in this rocky terrain and told her mother that she wanted to be a goatherd one day. Anything was better than becoming a nun, Van Hard replied. When it came time to leave the mountains and say goodbye to the goats, Sarah wept and pleaded. She wanted to take them with her to Grandchamp and saw no reason not to. In the end, weary of arguing, her mother purchased two nanny goats to graze on the convent grounds and give the girls milk.

Youle Van Hard was not alone in thinking that Sarah was unsuited to convent life. Mother Sainte Sophie agreed. Religious belief was not enough. A nun needed to practice obedience and bend her will to the service of others. Could Sarah keep her impulses under control? The answer became clear one afternoon when the students were hav-

Sarah flourished in the clean air and breathtaking landscape of the Pyrenees.

ing recess outdoors. Some soldiers stationed at nearby barracks were on the other side of the convent wall, horsing around. Suddenly a *shako*—a tall, rigid military hat—sailed over the wall and landed at Sarah's feet. A moment later, a soldier leaped onto the convent grounds and asked to have it back. But where had it gone? The giggling girls pretended not to know.

As if from nowhere, the hat appeared on Sarah's head. In a second, she had climbed a rope to the top beam of a tall piece of playground equipment, where no one could reach her, and pulled the rope up after her. She stood there in victory, with the shako falling over her eyes. What a commotion she caused! Officers from the barracks arrived, and together with Mother Sainte Sophie they pleaded with Sarah to return the soldier's hat. At last, shouting, "There it is, your shako!" Sarah tossed it so that it glided over a wall and into a cemetery. Then she refused to come down until everyone had gone away.

The soldiers left, and after a while the girls went indoors. The time came for Mother Sainte Sophie to resume her convent duties. Hours passed, dusk fell, and the air turned cold. Sarah grew hungry for her dinner, but still she remained on her perch. The gardener's big dog was prowling the grounds, and he frightened her. She felt relieved when she saw Mother Sainte Sophie returning. The caring nun convinced the headstrong girl that she would be safe.

No one knows whether the cause was exposure to cold or the lingering effects of pneumonia, but Sarah again got sick. This time she developed pleurisy, a painful inflammation of tissue surrounding the lungs. Youle Van Hard was traveling in Britain with a man and Aunt Rosine was in Germany, so Mother Sainte Sophie nursed Sarah. For more than three weeks, the devoted mother superior never left the girl's bedside. When Van Hard was back in France and Sarah had recovered enough, her mother took her home to Paris, having decided that Sarah's days at school were over.

Van Hard ordered her to forget that silly notion of becoming a nun, but Sarah argued back that she would never change her mind. To prove it, she hung pictures of saints in her bedroom and knelt beneath them in prayer for hours at a time. She wore her white confirmation dress day after day, with a string of rosary beads around her neck. The dress grew so filthy that it had to be thrown away. Youle produced tears at any mention of her daughter joining the sisters and made sure Sarah heard her noisy sobs.

Yet despite the discord, daily life went on. Because Sarah and her sisters still needed schooling and refinement, Van Hard hired a governess to come during the day and instruct her girls at home. Mademoiselle de Brabender was highly qualified, having once taught the children of Russian royalty. With graying hair and the shadow of a mustache, she was old enough to be Sarah's grandmother. Mademoiselle was a pious churchgoer, gentle and kind. As Sarah did whenever someone showed her affection, she gave Mademoiselle her loyalty and love. Van Hard also enrolled Sarah in art classes to perfect her ladylike accomplishments. Sarah had liked art lessons at the convent, and she continued to show talent. She won a prize for a painting she did of winter in Paris.

Living upstairs from Youle and her daughters was another person who gained Sarah's lasting friendship. Slim, dark-haired Madame Guérard was a young widow with children. She, too, was

Sophisticated and well connected, Charles Auguste Louis Joseph, duc de Morny, was to influence the course of Sarah's life.

devoted and sweet-natured. Sarah called her by an affectionate nickname, "my little lady."

One day in September 1859, as Sarah's fifteenth birthday neared, Youle Van Hard invited guests for lunch. Sarah's aunt Rosine came, and so did her godfather, Régis Lavolie, and Youle's close friend the duc de Morny. After the meal, Van Hard instructed Sarah to join the adults for coffee in the drawing room. It was a sunny space, decorated in green and yellow. There was not a speck of dirt on the carpet or dust on the potted plants, because Van Hard insisted on a spotless home. Others soon joined the company: Mademoiselle de Brabender, Sarah's uncle Félix Faure, and her little lady from upstairs, Madame Guérard. Once everyone had gathered and coffee was poured, Monsieur Lavolie rose. "As we have come here on account of this child," he said, "we must begin and discuss what is to be done with her."

Sarah understood all at once that her mother had called this meeting to decide her future. With panic in her eyes, she looked around at the adults in the room. What did they have in mind for her? It was "as though I was to be thrown into the sea," Bernhardt recalled, "when I could not swim."

TWO

France's Greatest Actor-in-Training

The art of acting is a vagrant art;
Its triumphs writ in water on the sands of time—
A perfect product of the brain and heart,
So quick disclosed, and so soon forgot . . .
—Anonymous, "To Sarah Bernhardt"

Youle Van Hard wanted to find Sarah a husband. Fifteen was young, but not too young for a girl legally to be a bride in nine-teenth-century France. Surely Sarah could attract a stable, hard-working man. She might marry a butcher, or maybe a clerk.

In urging Sarah to marry, Van Hard was looking out for herself as much as for her daughter. In the future, when men stopped paying for her company, she might need to rely on Sarah for support. But every-one in the apartment knew that a young lady looking to marry had to display feminine grace. She needed to be poised, demure, and refined. Sarah, with her noisy outbursts and religious fervor, fell far short of the ideal.

The talk went nowhere. Sarah insisted that she would marry her-self to the church, and the others told her it was out of the question. For such a strong-willed girl to take a vow of obedience would lead

to disaster, everyone agreed. Pretty soon the duc de Morny chimed in. "Do you know what you ought to do with this child?" he asked. "Send her to the Conservatoire."

"The Conservatoire!" Sarah recalled wondering. "What was it? What did it mean?" The duke explained that the Conservatoire, or National Conservatory, was a school for the performing arts. Many of its students studied music and dance under the finest teachers. The Conservatoire also trained actors for Paris's best theaters. A girl so full of feeling might find a home on the stage, Morny thought.

What nonsense, said Sarah's godfather, Régis Lavolie. "Why, she's as ugly as a louse!" Sarah, he went on to say, was "thin, undersized, always sick." He had a different idea: "apprentice her to a milliner!" Youle Van Hard rushed to Sarah's defense. Her oldest daughter had a wild streak, Van Hard admitted, but she was a charming girl, and any theater would be lucky to have her. Just look at those expressive eyes! A hatmaker? Not Sarah!

Nineteenth-century Parisians loved the theater more than any other form of entertainment. There were twenty theaters in the city and more in the surrounding suburbs. Throughout the year, they offered thousands of performances: comedies, tragedies, and tear-jerking melodramas. An actor under contract to an established theater earned a good, regular income.

Wife, milliner, actor. Sarah pictured herself in each role. She had been frightened when this meeting started, but at its close she felt empowered. "I had been discussed by every one," Bernhardt commented. "And now it was deemed necessary to humour and indulge me in order to win me over. They could not force me into agreeing to what they wanted me to do."

The persuasion began that very evening, when the adults took Sarah to the Comédie-Française. The renowned theater was near the

A French portrait photographer known as Nadar took this
picture of Sarah Bernhardt, age fifteen.

family's apartment in the rue Saint-Honoré. Sarah often saw its actors on the sidewalk on their way to work, and sometimes she spoke to them. Now she was about to watch those actors onstage.

Sarah took a seat. The curtain rose, the crowd hushed, and she was spellbound. That night the company performed two plays. The first, a tragedy, left Sarah in tears. The second play was a comedy based on Greek mythology—and it, too, made Sarah cry. She missed all the humor because she felt so sorry for one character, a faithful wife who

The Comédie-Française presented classical French drama in a glorious setting.

was tricked by the gods. Her loud boohooing amused strangers in the seats around her, but not her mortified mother and governess. Youle Van Hard and Mademoiselle de Brabender hurried her down the aisle and out the door.

The evening was cut short, but every sight and sound had imprinted itself on Sarah's mind. As time went on and she told and retold the story of that night, she added details that came straight from her imagination. She sometimes said, for example, that the famous playwright Alexandre Dumas *père* (father, or senior) had accompanied the group home and tucked her into bed that night.

The day after the trip to the Comédie-Française, Sarah paged through her old textbooks to find the dramatic speeches she used to recite for her friends at boarding school: "If my rival I embrace, it is to crush him!" "Tyrant, why leave thy butchery half done?" She memorized them all. Sarah believed she had found a new direction in life. Instead of becoming a nun, she would study at the Conservatoire— although her mother still hoped that she might be some steadfast man's wife.

Very well; the duc de Morny arranged for her to have an audition. As the half brother of France's reigning emperor, Napoleon III, the duke had influence. He served as president of the *Corps législatif*, the national legislature, and had thriving business interests. He owned valuable racehorses and paintings, and he had friends in the theatrical world. At forty-eight, he was trim and balding, with a neat mustache and goatee. He dressed elegantly, always with a drop of perfume on his handkerchief.

Sarah had a month to prepare. She practiced a scene from *The School for Wives*, a comedy by the seventeenth-century dramatist Molière. On the day of the audition, she walked into the Conservatoire with Mademoiselle de Brabender and her little lady, Madame Guérard. Many girls and boys were already there with their parents. One by one, they were summoned before the examiners to try out for the prestigious school. At last it was Sarah's turn. She was ushered into the audition room, where she told the esteemed faculty which scene she planned to perform. They asked who would be cueing her, and Sarah looked confused. They then explained that she was supposed to have brought another person who was prepared to act the scene with her, to recite the lines said by other characters.

Oh, no! Sarah had not been told about this and had no one to cue her. There was no way she could present her scene. Thinking fast, she offered to recite an old fable about two doves, which she knew by heart from childhood. What? "Is this a joke?" a teacher asked. "This isn't a nursery school!"

Not knowing what else to do, Sarah repeated the tale, which French children learned when they were little: "Two Doves, twin-brothers of a nest, / By tender friendship's flame possest . . . Neither abroad desir'd to roam; / Till one at length, grew sick of home . . ." But what came next? Her mind had gone blank. She looked fearfully from one waiting face to another.

Take your time; try again, said the director of the school. So Sarah began anew, and this time she remembered all the words. *Très bien*, she was told. As she turned to leave, the director asked a final question: "Are you a Jewess?" He had heard a rumor about her mother. Sarah answered, "By birth, sir, but I have been baptized." The director remarked to his colleagues, "She's been baptized, and it would have been a pity for such a pretty child not to be."

In 1791, France became only the second European country, after Poland, to grant Jews equality as citizens. Jews in France could hold elected office and attend universities, things they were barred from doing in other parts of Europe. For this reason, Jews had been immigrating to France, which they viewed as a land of opportunity. But even with immigration, they made up a small segment of France's population. Many French Christians had never met a Jewish person, and many held anti-Semitic views. It was common for French Christians to believe that Jews were inferior people or that the Jewish faith was less advanced than their own. Some thought that Jews were profiting at the expense of their non-Jewish neighbors. Jews were often subject to insults and discrimination.

One day Sarah Bernhardt would claim her Jewish heritage with pride. For the moment, she was simply relieved that the audition was over. Some one hundred hopeful young people had tried out for the two-year program, but no more than twenty would be accepted.

Outside the Conservatoire, nervous applicants and their chaperones wait to learn who has been accepted into the exclusive school.

Despite her less-than-stellar performance, Sarah was one of them. "I was mad with joy," she said, and she rushed home to tell her mother. Van Hard, Régis Lavolie, and Aunt Rosine pretended to be surprised and congratulated Sarah on her success.

In years to come, Bernhardt liked to say that her golden voice and clear diction won over the faculty, but she also admitted much later in life that at fifteen she had a bad habit of talking through clenched teeth. In truth, it was the duc de Morny's influence that gained Sarah a place at the school.

Students at the Conservatoire learned to act in the grand style preferred by the Comédie-Française. They were taught to use gestures to show what a character thought or felt. They might put a hand to their forehead when a character was thinking. A soulful gaze meant that a person was feeling sentimental. Because many classical plays featured lofty figures—kings and queens or gods and goddesses—actors copied the stances of ancient statues. They also practiced the graceful poses of people in paintings. At its best, this method of acting presented the audience with a pretty picture. At its worst, it was dull and predictable. A critic of the grand style wrote that anyone watching one well-known actor could tell "by the extension of one arm, when to expect an *Ah!* and by the brandishing of the other when to expect an *Oh!*"

The students had lessons on how to stand and walk: "throw the body back, hold up the head, walk on tip-toes. That's right. One, two, three, march." Walking one way showed that a character was careless; walking another way conveyed dignity, or perhaps rage. Then there were all the different ways of sitting: falling heavily into a chair, for example, or leaning forward to show interest. Hardest for Sarah was sitting ironically. "Oh, that one!" she recalled. "Mouth raised on one side, laughter in the eyes, and imperceptible shrugging of the shoulders." The students also had rules to memorize, such as never to stand with their back to the audience when speaking. Opinion was divided

A class at the Conservatoire. Some students perform while others look on.

as to how they were supposed to say their lines. French dramatists of earlier centuries wrote their plays in verse, as William Shakespeare had done. Actors could chant their lines, stressing the rhythm and rhyme of the poetry. Or they could let the words flow naturally, as people would say them in real life.

Sarah's principal teacher, Jean-Baptiste Provost, was a leading actor in the Comédie-Française. He was an excellent instructor when it came to analyzing a script and discussing why a scene worked. When the class had to act out that scene, though, he was inflexible. The only students who earned his approval were the ones who copied his own broad movements. He had no patience with someone who wanted to be creative and try out new ideas.

What was he to make of the student he called "little rebel," this untamed girl who rushed in late to class? Sarah walked to school every morning so she could keep the coins her mother gave her for the horse-drawn omnibus. She never missed a lesson, but Provost never could say he liked her. She irritated him and left him frustrated. At the same time, he saw some quality in her, some untested talent. If only he could draw it out! For this reason, he was harder on Sarah than on others in his class. Coaching her on a scene from *Zaïre*, a classical tragedy by the great eighteenth-century writer Voltaire, he corrected every gesture she made. Bernhardt was playing the title character, an enslaved woman who wins a sultan's heart only to arouse his murderous jealousy. It was a demanding role with a dramatic death scene. Provost fine-tuned changes in the pitch and tone of Sarah's voice. When the time came for the sword that would kill her to be drawn, he ordered her to shout and show stormy rage. But Sarah resisted, and he got nowhere with her. After two hours he threw up his hands, saying, "There's a role you have to remember never to play."

Sarah could have obeyed Provost—if she had wanted to. She had her own ideas about how the scene should be played, and she thought that her teacher's way was wrong. Sarah, too, saw potential in herself. She believed that if she worked hard enough, she could be the greatest actor in France. She would come to see that artists can learn only so much from their teachers. To master any kind of creative work, a person must make a solitary journey. Watching, listening, practicing, making mistakes, and thinking for herself were necessary steps in Sarah's artistic growth.

The months of study passed quickly. At the end of the year, instead of taking a final exam, the students each performed two scenes, one from a tragedy and another from a comedy, and the teachers awarded prizes to those who did best. On this momentous day, the students' families crammed the courtyard of the Conservatoire. The crowd was thickest outside the small door that led to the room where the students performed.

For her tragic piece, Sarah chose the scene from *Zaïre* that had frustrated Monsieur Provost. This time she went against Provost's teaching and acted the scene as she thought it should be done. Instead of ending in violent anger, she introduced tenderness. "I fell on my knees," she wrote, "with a sob so real, my arms outstretched, offering my heart, so full of love, to the deadly blow that I expected."

Sarah Bernhardt was sometimes at odds with Jean-Baptiste Provost,
her demanding teacher.

When all the scenes had been performed, the esteemed faculty emerged from the room. Then the students came out, some with ashen faces, others looking buoyant. They found their loved ones and announced their results. Sarah's daring effort won her second prize in tragedy, and in comedy she received honorable mention. She believed her tragic scene had been the best, but as a first-year student, she was satisfied. "It was only just that I should have the second, on account of my age and the short time I had been studying," she said. If Monsieur Provost witnessed her performance, he kept his opinion to himself.

The next year, she set her heart on winning a first prize at the final performances, but things went horribly wrong from the start. Certain that Sarah would never get ahead unless she did something with her frizzy hair, Youle Van Hard took her to a hairdresser. He greased Sarah's hair with pomade, twisted it around hot curling irons, and pinned it up. "I looked perfectly hideous," Sarah stated. "My hair was drawn tightly back from my temples, my ears were very visible and stood out, looking positively bold in their bareness, whilst on top of my head was a parcel of little sausages." She showed up at the Conservatoire on performance day looking like a different girl, with a face swollen from crying. Friends helped her pull the many pins out of her hairdo, and the sausages fell around her face.

Sarah knew she looked peculiar, and crying had left her with a stuffy nose. Her voice sounded like someone else's, but she got through her tragic scene as well as she could. As she made her bow, she heard someone say, "Poor child; she ought not to have been allowed to compete. She has an atrocious cold." She had time to calm down before her comedic scene, but her performance was far from her best. She received second prize for comedy and nothing at all for tragedy.

It was a disappointing way to end her time at the Conservatoire. And she worried about where she would go from there. Only the top students were invited to join the Comédie-Française, and Sarah had not been one of them. It hardly helped to be picked on by her godfather. "You were a failure. Why persist now in going on the stage?" he asked her. "You are thin and small, your face is pretty enough when near, but ugly in the distance." This time her mother said nothing in her defense; Sarah had failed in Van Hard's eyes too.

That night, Sarah went to bed early, under a heavy blanket of sadness. "Had there been any poison at hand I would have taken it," Bernhardt said. She woke in the night to discover a note that had been placed on her bedside table. It was from Madame Guérard, and it contained good news. Her engagement at the Comédie-Française was confirmed. "Do not worry any more, therefore, my dear child," Sarah read, "but have faith in the future."

Again the duc de Morny had stepped in to help Sarah. She had hoped to be accepted on her own merits, but since that had not happened, she would try to deserve the opportunity she had been given. No, she was going to do better than that. One way or another, Sarah Bernhardt would triumph.

THREE

STEPPING ONTO THE WORLD'S STAGE

Those amazingly blue eyes, widely-spaced; that arched nose,
a pulse beating in the sensitive nostril as she talked;
that glorious mouth, full and red, the upper lip slightly
projecting over the under one . . . Many another face
I might see and forget, this one, never!
—Thérèse Berton, actor's wife

The next day, Sarah was to meet with Édouard Thierry, director of the Comédie-Française. Her mother and aunt Rosine rummaged through her closet, tossing aside one dress after another. Sarah's clothes were all too childish, the women decided. They forced her to wear a grown-up dress of her aunt's that was the color of cabbage. Sarah felt like a trained monkey made to wear a garish costume.

The meeting was brief. Thierry gave Sarah a contract for her mother to sign, because Sarah herself was still a minor. As a beginner, she was to receive fifty francs a month, a little more than a housemaid earned. Still, she would be able to pay something toward her own support, as Youle Van Hard insisted she do. And if Sarah failed to contribute? Well, Van Hard could count three men—a glove maker, a tanner, and a druggist—who might be inclined to marry. "My mother isn't married herself, yet she wants me to be a wife," Sarah commented. She vowed that if she ever did marry, it would be for love alone.

Despite its name, the Comédie-Française staged both comedies and tragedies. It was founded in 1680 by King Louis XIV to ensure that the great dramas written during his reign would be kept alive. By tradition, the Comédie-Française showcased new actors by casting them in three plays. These debuts were a chance for the players to show audiences what they could do. If the public liked them, then they were assured of a promising future with the company.

Sarah Bernhardt made her first debut on September 1, 1862, starring in a drama based on mythology. She played a king's daughter, a maiden willing to give her life for her father and nation. That night, she got to the theater early. She put on the costume chosen for her, which she thought looked awful, and applied her makeup. A little while later, standing in the wings, she sensed the return of her old enemy, stage fright. How good it was, then, at that moment, to hear a familiar voice from behind her. It belonged to her old teacher, Monsieur Provost, who was performing later that night. He told her to be confident, and when it was time for her entrance, he gave her a quick little shove onto the stage. Sarah brushed aside her fear and did her best. But was her best good enough?

Plays presented at the Comédie-Française were reviewed in the press. The critic who wrote about this one noted that Mademoiselle Bernhardt was a slender girl with a nice face. "She holds herself well, and her enunciation is perfectly clear," he added. "That's all that can be said for her at the moment." He ignored her second debut, several days later. About her third, in a classical comedy, he wrote, "This performance was a very poor business."

"I was insignificant," Sarah believed. She was crushed after reading the reviews, and her mother's berating hardly helped. "See! The whole world calls you stupid," Youle Van Hard sneered, "and the whole world knows that you're my child!"

Most evenings, to avoid her mother's sharp tongue, Sarah ate dinner in the nursery with Mademoiselle de Brabender and her sister Régine. She adored this headstrong little girl with big blue eyes. She spoiled her, saying yes to her whims when she should have said no. Sometimes she brought the child to the Comédie-Française and let her sit through rehearsals.

Wearing period costumes, actors employed by the Comédie-Française present a play by the seventeenth-century dramatist Molière.

Every January 15, the troupe held a ceremony to mark the birth in 1622 of the great Molière. All the actors lined up to walk onstage and honor a bust of the revered playwright. At home, Sarah talked about this custom and how she would take part for the first time. Régine, who was listening, begged to come along. *Please! Oh, please!* She promised to keep quiet and hold her big sister's hand. What could Sarah do? She hated to see Régine unhappy.

That night the actors—and Régine—assembled in the theater's foyer. At a signal, they moved forward, and as they did, the little girl stepped on the hem of another performer's gown. This performer was none other than Mademoiselle Nathalie, who believed herself to be an important person. The daunting woman spun around and with one powerful arm threw Régine against a marble pillar. It was a sudden, violent act that left Régine bleeding and in tears. Immediately Sarah flew to her sister's defense. "You miserable creature!" she cried, and she slapped Nathalie's cheek as hard as she could.

The procession broke down as the senior actors crowded around Nathalie, who had momentarily fainted. Someone poured water on Nathalie's face, causing her to blubber, "You'll spoil my make-up!" The younger players tended to Régine, whose strong voice rang out as well. "I did not do it on purpose," Régine cried. "She's an old cow." The troupe at last made it onto the stage, twenty minutes late.

The next day, Édouard Thierry summoned Sarah to his office and tried to smooth things over. If Sarah apologized to Mademoiselle Nathalie, he said, he would ask the theater's administrators to be lenient with her. She did not have to be fired; maybe she could simply pay a fine and remain with the Comédie-Française. But Sarah was not sorry, and she refused to say that she was. It seemed to her that if anyone should apologize, it was Nathalie. Sarah spoke impulsively. "I will leave; I will cancel my engagement at once," she said. Thierry told her

Mademoiselle Nathalie was an established actor and Sarah Bernhardt was still a novice when they clashed at the Comédie-Française.

that quitting was a mistake, but her mind was made up, even as she saw her dream of greatness fading to nothing. She thought about the people at home. Her mother would be furious at her for throwing away this opportunity; her aunt and godfather were sure to make fun of her. "I thought too of my beloved Brabender," Bernhardt wrote, "with her hands clasped, her moustache drooping sadly, her small eyes full of tears." Yet, knowing full well the consequences of her action, Sarah tore her contract into little pieces.

For days she avoided her glowering mother. She escaped upstairs whenever she could to be with Madame Guérard, who taught her to make hot chocolate and scrambled eggs. One snowy day when she was at home and Régis Lavolie was expected for lunch, Sarah sensed that something was up. Her mother and her sister Jeanne were acting mysteriously, as if they knew a secret. Sure enough, when her godfather arrived, he handed Sarah a letter. "Here, read that, you self-willed girl," he said.

The page bore the heading of the Gymnase, a theater that presented "drawing-room comedies," lighthearted plays about wealthy people living glamorous lives. The letter was from the theater's manager, who was offering Sarah a job—as a favor to Lavolie. Sarah was astonished: her crude, faultfinding godfather had done something nice for her. Word of her behavior at the Comédie-Française had gotten around, though. The manager mentioned that her "vile temper" caused him to have misgivings.

Sarah took the job with gratitude and vowed to keep her anger in check. She played small parts at the Gymnase and was an understudy for actors in leading roles. During this apprenticeship, she fell in love for the first time, with Charles Joseph Eugène Henri, prince de Ligne, a wealthy Belgian nobleman. In later years, Bernhardt told differing stories about how the two met. According to one, they encountered each other when actors from the Gymnase were performing for the emperor. The prince stepped forward to defend Sarah when the company's director publicly scolded her for a mistake. In another version, they met at a masked ball when Sarah traveled to Belgium in summer 1863. The prince, enchanted, gave her a rose.

Love was magical, but Sarah still had to show up for rehearsals. At work she kept her temper under control, and in spring she was assigned a larger part to play. She should have been happy, but she disliked the role. The play, she thought, was stupid, and her character, a Russian princess, was an idiot, always laughing, eating, or dancing. Sarah moved sullenly through rehearsals, with the result that on opening night no one liked her performance. She felt keenly disappointed in herself. And, as usual, Youle Van Hard had hurtful things to say: "My poor child, you were ridiculous in your Russian princess *rôle,* and I was very much grieved!"

Early the next morning, after a sleepless night, Sarah trotted upstairs to Madame Guérard's apartment and asked for a bottle of laudanum. In the 1800s, Europeans used this opium-based drug to treat all kinds of ailments, from headaches to coughs and upset stomachs. Guérard suspected that her distraught friend had a darker purpose in mind, and a few apt questions revealed that she was right. Sarah was planning to swallow all the laudanum and take her own life. Guérard, of course, refused the request. She calmed the girl down (or so she thought) and sent her home.

But Sarah was in turmoil, feeling trapped and needing to escape. Since she was not going to die, she would run away. The next day at dawn, she was back at Guérard's door to say that she was going to Spain. *Come with me, my little lady,* she begged. Madame Guérard reminded Sarah that her children needed her at home. So Sarah woke another neighbor, named Caroline, who had worked as a dressmaker for Youle Van Hard, and convinced her to come along as a maid.

Sarah packed some clothes and a small statue of the Virgin Mary. Taking money she had saved and borrowing more from Madame Guérard, she sneaked out of the apartment before anyone else was awake. She left a note for her mother, and, stopping at the Gymnase, she dropped off another one for the management. "Have pity on a poor, crazy girl!" it read.

Sarah and Caroline took a train to the southern port of Marseilles and boarded a dirty boat that smelled of fish. Six days later they reached Alicante, on the Spanish coast, where a calm bay reflected the surrounding mountains. They took a room in the first hotel they passed but soon knew they had made a mistake. This rough stone inn sheltered men on the move and rarely welcomed ladies as guests. Sarah, used to clean, perfumed bedding at home, could not bring herself to undress and sleep on the hotel's soiled sheets. After a man peeked into the women's room in the wee hours of the morning, Sarah and Caroline had the innkeeper send for the police.

Someone fetched a Hungarian diplomat who spoke French to help the officers question the two women. When the investigation was complete, he invited Sarah and Caroline to stay in his home. The grateful women were soon drinking *café au lait* with the diplomat

Sarah and Caroline stayed first in Alicante, on the Spanish coast.

In bright, sunny Madrid, Sarah imagined a life free from cares. "I forgot Paris, my sorrows, disappointments, ambitions, and everything else," she wrote. "I wanted to live in Spain."

and his wife. A few days later they moved on to sunbaked Madrid, in central Spain. They found rooms at a good hotel, and Sarah sent a message to her family. Then she and Caroline explored the city. They went to bullfights; they walked past stables that smelled of horse dung, and food shops spilling the aromas of cheese and sausages into the street.

After two weeks, a telegram arrived from Madame Guérard, informing Sarah that her mother was gravely ill. The travelers caught a train back to Paris, where Sarah found Van Hard in bed with pleurisy but already getting well. "My mother looked very white, lying in her bed," Bernhardt remembered. "Her face was thinner, but wonderfully beautiful." Mother and daughter had a tearful reunion. Sarah learned from Van Hard that her grandmother—her father's mother—was releasing some money to her. This meant that Sarah, now nineteen, could live independently. She and her mother could never share a home peacefully, Sarah knew.

Before long, Sarah informed her family that she was renting a flat nearby, in the rue Duphot. "Take me with you this time!" pleaded Régine, age nine, who had been sad when Sarah went to Spain without her. Before Sarah could respond, their mother said, "Oh, take her, for she is unbearable."

For years Sarah had watched Van Hard favor Jeanne over little Régine, and she had felt their mother's coldness herself. But now, hearing Van Hard reject her youngest child, "I was perfectly stupefied," Bernhardt said. She welcomed her sister into her home. She hired a maid to help care for her, and Madame Guérard promised to visit often.

Someone else would soon join the household in the rue Duphot, because Sarah was going to have a baby. In truth, she had discovered the pregnancy just before dashing off to Alicante in distress.

Maurice Bernhardt was born on December 22, 1864, and Sarah informed the prince de Ligne that he had a son. As a man of noble birth, he was unlikely to marry an actor, but Sarah hoped that he would provide for Maurice, as her own father had done for her. Instead he sent her fifty francs and a curt note: "I know a woman named Bernhardt, but I do not know her child." Sarah understood that he was through with her. To her prince, she had been an amusement and nothing more.

For a girl from a conventional family, bearing an illegitimate child was a great shame. It ruined her reputation, destroyed her chances of marriage, and possibly caused her loved ones to reject her. Hoping to keep their pregnancies secret, many young women disappeared into the streets of Paris. There they gave birth, alone and friendless, and often surrendered their babies to institutions called hospices. These places cared for abandoned infants, but they were overcrowded, dirty, and dangerous for little ones. Half of all foundlings entering Paris hospices died in their first year of life.

Things were different in the demimonde, where illegitimacy barely raised an eyebrow. Nor did it matter to Sarah Bernhardt, who had grown up as the daughter of a single woman. She would proudly acknowledge Maurice as her son, and unlike Youle Van Hard, she was determined to be a loving, devoted mother. She found a motto for life in an everyday expression, *quand même*, which means "all the same" or "even so." No matter the challenges that life presented, Bernhardt would keep going. Whether she faced good luck or misfortune, it made no difference: *quand même*.

The question was, how would she support her little family? The money from her grandmother stretched just so far, and Sarah had already spent much of it on pretty furniture and ornaments that caught her eye. During the past months, pregnancy and early motherhood had kept her from acting and bringing home her pay. Van Hard had helped by feeding Sarah and Régine dinner at her table each evening, for which Sarah was grateful. For a time, she followed her mother's example, letting men pay her for companionship and sex. Her clients included a retired military officer, a Spanish nobleman, an Egyptian diplomat, and a wealthy banker, among others. Some nights, after the children were put to bed, they turned her small parlor into their salon, the space where they got together and talked.

But Sarah was unhappy; this was not how she wanted to live. If only she could get back onstage! With nothing to lose, she wrote to a gentleman who knew her mother and aunt. He was Camille Doucet, head of the Theater Department in the government's Ministry of Fine Arts. He arranged for Sarah to meet the new managers of the Odéon

Theater, who were looking for fresh faces to add to their company. Doucet spoke frankly to Sarah. "You've got to calm down and stop wasting your talents. No more rushing around and running away and slapping people," he said. "Everyone knows how hard you are to control, and I've had to swear you'll be as gentle as a lamb."

Gentle as a lamb? Sarah Bernhardt? She easily charmed the first of the Odéon's directors, Félix Duquesnel, who sent her to see his partner, Charles de Chilly. This gentleman, who had a contract for Bernhardt to sign, was less impressed. "You know, it's Duquesnel who's responsible for your being here," he said. "There's no way I would have taken you on." Bernhardt swiftly responded, "And if it had been you alone, monsieur, I wouldn't have signed." But she did sign, and with a nursemaid watching the children at home, she returned to work. Maurice grew up in servants' care, much as Bernhardt did before she

As the single mother of a young son, Bernhardt was grateful
to find employment at the Odéon.

went to school. No one accused Bernhardt of neglecting her son, however. Instead, some people thought that she pampered and indulged him. He wore fine clothes and owned any toy he wished for. When he was old enough, Bernhardt made sure he always had plenty of spending money.

The Comédie-Française and the Odéon were both national theaters, but the Odéon was newer and less renowned. The two theaters attracted different audiences: older folk tended to prefer the Comédie-Française, but young adults flocked to the Odéon. The people filling most seats at the Comédie-Française had been going there for years. They went to see classical plays performed as they always had been, according to tradition. "Oh those traditions!" Bernhardt groaned. "How many enthusiastic and sincere actors have found themselves fettered by them." The atmosphere was freer at the Odéon. There, "we only breathed dreams," Bernhardt said. "We did not walk; we hovered with wings."

Bernhardt's first performances at the Odéon drew little attention. Chilly wanted to fire her, but Duquesnel urged patience. Sarah needed time to practice her craft and learn to use the gifts that he believed she possessed. Sarah worked hard, and gradually audiences and critics took notice. She became a favorite of students at the Sorbonne, the great university in Paris. Her fans called themselves *Saradoteurs*.

Sarah Bernhardt had been with the Odéon for less than two years when Duquesnel and Chilly decided to stage *Ruy Blas*, a play by the noted writer Victor Hugo. As soon as they announced their choice, they received a swift warning from the government. It seemed that *Ruy Blas* contained a call for political reform that was offensive to Emperor Napoleon III. Also Hugo, author of the great novel *Les Misérables* and other important works, had spoken out publicly against the current leadership. He had called the emperor a traitor to France for seizing power in a coup d'état in 1851. Because of his views, Hugo was voluntarily living in exile on the island of Guernsey. When the government insisted that the Odéon withdraw *Ruy Blas,* Duquesnel and Chilly complied. They substituted *Kean,* by Alexandre Dumas *père.* Based on the life of Edmund Kean, a British actor of an earlier generation, this drama was a safer choice. Bernhardt was given the leading female role.

The switch angered many Parisians, who accused the theater's managers of lacking courage. On opening night, in February 1868, protesters descended on the Odéon, ready for a fight. They chanted, *Ruy Blas!* Victor Hugo!

The demonstrators in the audience shouted in anger as the curtain rose. But when Bernhardt stepped onstage, the Saradoteurs cheered and clapped, giving her the courage she needed to deliver her lines. Then, as the first scene came to its close, a large group of protesters, as many as sixty, gathered in the aisle, locked arms, and marched toward the stage. Things were getting out of hand, but if Bernhardt felt fear, she mastered it. She stepped forward, and her musical voice rang out: "Do you think you are encouraging justice by holding Alexandre Dumas responsible for Victor Hugo's exile?" People paused to listen, and as they closed their mouths and stood still, they gained control of themselves. The performance of *Kean* went on, and Sarah Bernhardt was hailed as the hero of the night.

A year later, Bernhardt starred in a new play set during the Renaissance. In *Le Passant,* she portrayed a traveling minstrel, a young lute player called Zanetto. This was the first of several male roles that Bernhardt would take on. Passing through Florence, Italy, Zanetto warms the heart of a hardened old courtesan named Sylvia. Zanetto vows to remain with Sylvia, but she insists that he resume his wandering. The two part, and with his new knowledge of love, Zanetto strums his lute with greater feeling.

Bernhardt shone in this simple play. She was sprightly and charming, and her voice was as clear as a chime. The playwright, François Coppée, was full of praise. "What can be said of Sarah, so thin, so svelte . . . whose entire being had the suppleness, the lightness, the grace of a youth?" he asked. "What intoxication, what joy, what childish folly in my Zanetto!" The public could not get enough of her. So many people wanted to see *Le Passant* that the Odéon presented it one hundred and fifty times. The players were even summoned to the Tuileries Palace to give a command performance for the emperor and empress.

Sarah Bernhardt had finally become the star everyone wanted to see. She was always on the go, sometimes stopping at home just to change her clothes or grab a bite. Her maid slacked off, and as a result the apartment looked sloppy and thrown together. Plates of half-eaten food lay about, the children's things were left here and there, and dust covered the furniture and knickknacks. Sarah's pet tortoises, Chrysagère and Zerbinette, wandered through the mess. Chrysagère wore a jeweled, golden shell that fit over his natural one. The smaller Zerbinette followed him like a servant. Sarah delighted in them.

One night, Bernhardt was having dinner in her apartment with some guests. It was late, and everyone else in the household had gone to bed. Sarah and her company were relaxing after their meal when they heard shouts from the street below: Fire! They looked out to see people pointing and calling, trying to get their attention. Smoke was coming from Sarah's building, they said. In fact, flames could be seen through the window of Sarah's bedchamber! The fire was right there, in her apartment. Sarah rushed to the bedrooms. She picked up a sleeping Maurice, woke the maids and Régine, and hurried them all downstairs and into a shop across the street as flames swept through the rooms.

Bernhardt first earned critical acclaim in the role of Zanetto.

Firefighters determined that a lighted candle left near a lace bed-curtain had started the blaze. All the people were safe, but nothing in the apartment could be salvaged. Chrysagère and Zerbinette were dead. "I was absolutely ruined," Bernhardt said. She had no choice, though, but to go on. *Quand même.*

FOUR

UNDER SIEGE

You are lauded now as fair,
Lovely, gay, bewitching, rare,
Chic, entrancing, debonair,
Shy, petite.
And, like gulls along the shore
Fly admirers to the door . . .
—Anonymous, "To Sara B."

What was she going to do? The landlord's insurance company was demanding that Bernhardt pay to repair the building. The company wanted forty thousand francs, an impossible sum. Luckily, Félix Duquesnel stepped in to help. Bernhardt's boss planned a benefit performance at the Odéon, with all profits going toward her bills. When the opera star Adelina Patti agreed to sing, Sarah felt relieved. Patti always drew crowds, and soon every ticket was sold. For Patti's fans, the benefit show was unforgettable. They applauded so much for one aria that the popular singer sang it three times. Bernhardt paid the insurance company with profits from the evening, but she still had lost everything she owned.

She moved her family into the best place she could afford, a shabby flat in a dismal old building, and thought hard about what to do. She had been invited to join an acting company in Russia that would pay her generously. Bernhardt hated the idea of leaving Paris for such a cold, distant place, but she was desperate to get back on her feet. She had just about decided to take the job when a lawyer representing her father's estate came to call. He informed Sarah that her grandmother had read in a newspaper about the fire and was releasing more money to her. Life, as always, was full of surprises. "How differently things turn out from what seems likely according to logic or according to our own expectations," Sarah reflected. She forgot all about Russia and rented a first-floor apartment in a sunny Paris house.

With her life back on track, Bernhardt plunged into her work at the Odéon. She was to star as a young girl in *L'Autre,* a new drama by one of France's most popular women writers. This novelist and playwright was known by her pen name, George Sand. She was a famous romantic rebel who had had many lovers, among them the composer Frédéric Chopin. She smoked cigars and sometimes wore men's clothing to disguise herself in public. Now in her seventies, Sand was nearing the end of her life. Her posture was stooped, and she had developed a double chin. Bernhardt admired her large eyes, so deep with feeling, and her gentle voice. Still yearning for a mother's love, she often sat beside this fabled older woman and held her hand.

Sand was directing her own play, and as she watched the actors rehearse, she worried. "They do well, all but Sarah," she wrote in the journal she was keeping. She wondered if Sarah might be lazy or stupid. It annoyed her when Sarah took off for several days to nurse her sister Jeanne, who had suffered a miscarriage. (Jeanne, who was not yet twenty, already had a daughter named Saryta, and had fallen into a life of prostitution and drug abuse.) People who knew Bernhardt assured Sand that she would calm down and learn her part, and they were

George Sand, author of many novels and plays, was one of Europe's most popular writers. She was nearing the end of her career when she worked with Sarah Bernhardt.

right. Before long, Sand could write, "Everyone's acting has improved, Sarah's most of all."

When the show opened, reviewers singled out Bernhardt for praise: "Young and charming, Bernhardt projects the chaste and audacious quality of a real girl who knows nothing, fears nothing, and reproaches herself with nothing." To play her character, Bernhardt reached back in memory and felt again the emotions of a girl on the cusp of womanhood. She drew on her courage, which she had gained through experience.

Bernhardt's popularity was growing, and her reputation was spreading. But in the world of Sarah Bernhardt, life never progressed smoothly. Sure enough, in summer 1870, while resting in the south of France with Maurice and enjoying her success, she learned that her country was at war with German states to the east.

Germany was not one country at the time but several separate kingdoms and principalities, each with its own ruling family. In 1866, a few of these states had formed a confederation. In so doing, they gained strength and upset the balance of power in Europe. As the Germans' influence rose, France's declined. What would happen, the French worried, if more German states united?

Germany's military forces outnumbered France's. They were better trained and employed more advanced technology. French leaders knew all this. Nevertheless, on July 16, 1870, wanting to secure its dominance in Europe, France declared war on the German kingdom of Prussia— and brought on disaster. Armies from Prussia and other German states swept into France and won battle after battle. On September 4, Napoleon III fell from power. France's National Assembly hurriedly formed a new government, headed briefly by an army general and then by a president selected by the assembly. All the while, the catastrophic war went on.

Was there any safe place in France? Country people fled their homes before German troops destroyed them, and poured into Paris. Thousands of Parisians packed up and left the city, fearing it was only a matter of time until Paris came under attack. Many of their neighbors denied that an assault on the beautiful city was even possible. "The capture of Paris seemed to us such a monstrous sacrilege," wrote one city resident, "that it didn't enter our imagination that this crime could be accomplished."

To be ready for a possible siege, the authorities strengthened fortifications around the city. They blocked or destroyed roads and bridges

Sarah Bernhardt's son, Maurice, would always be the most important person in her life.

leading into Paris and barricaded the river Seine. They brought in food, including a quarter million sheep and forty thousand head of cattle. Some animals were butchered right away, but others grazed in public spaces. An English journalist reported that "as far as ever the eye can reach, over every open space" he saw "nothing but sheep, sheep, sheep!" The Louvre and other museums moved priceless artworks out of Paris or stored them away in cellars.

Bernhardt hurried back to Paris with one thought in mind: keeping her family safe. She had left Régine in the care of her aunts. Now she gathered up all her loved ones and brought them to a railroad station. There, she paid their fare to Holland. She forced her way to the head of a line of passengers holding tickets and pushed her mother, her sisters, her niece Saryta, and her aunts onto the train. Lastly, she said goodbye to Maurice. Sarah hated to part from her son, not knowing when she might see him again, but she needed to get him far away from danger. As for herself, she was going to stay and help her country. "I decided to use my strength and intelligence in tending the wounded," she explained.

The police had ordered all theaters in Paris to close, but the Comédie-Française had reopened as a hospital for wounded soldiers. Bernhardt thought about the Odéon, with its doors locked and its stage dark and silent. She asked herself, why not turn it into a hospital too? Thousands of suffering men had been transported into Paris from battles elsewhere. Knowing that if a siege started, there would be many more, she sprang into action. Duquesnel told her that she could use the theater, and the government's War Office gave her the permission she needed. Wasting no time, Bernhardt brought in workers to clear the building of furnishings to make room for cots and medical equipment. The lobby, auditorium, stage, and dressing rooms became wards. She called on friends and merchants to provide food and supplies. They gave her everything from eggs, coffee, and biscuits to bed linens and nightshirts. She turned her apartment into a chicken coop

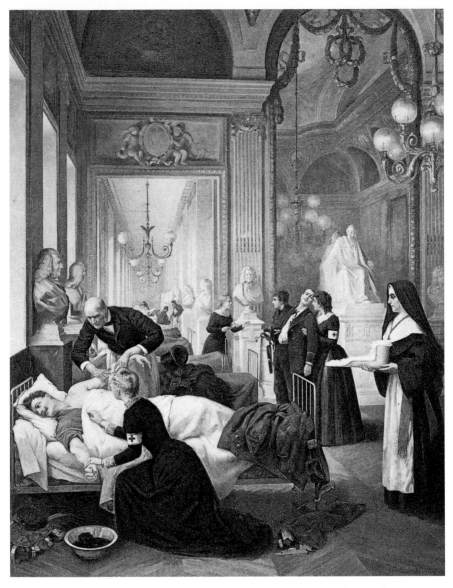

Like the Odéon, the Comédie-Française served as a hospital
during the Franco-Prussian War.

so that she could accept a gift of forty hens and six geese. Bernhardt
planned to live at the hospital and care for the soldiers herself. Some
women from the acting community offered to assist her, among them
Marie Colombier, an old friend from the Conservatoire. Dear Madame
Guérard was also on hand to help.

And the war went on. By September 19, two hundred thousand Prussian fighting men surrounded Paris. They waited only for their big guns to arrive, and then the bombardment would begin. The Germans expected the assault to be brief. The Parisians were too fond of comfort to hold out for long, they told themselves. Paris was sure to give up after "eight days without *café au lait*," joked Prussia's leader, Otto von Bismarck.

Captives in their own city, Parisians kept hoping for French forces to show up and attack the Germans from the outside, but this never happened. Day after day, Paris's food supply dwindled. Weeks passed, and fresh vegetables and milk were nowhere to be found. Cheese, someone said, was just a memory. Once the livestock was consumed, people butchered horses, dogs, cats, exotic animals from the zoo, and even rodents. "This morning I regaled myself with a rat *pâté*," one man admitted, "which wasn't bad at all." During the coldest winter in twenty years, people stood in line for hours to get a bowl of soup.

Meanwhile, the enemy strengthened its position. On January 6, 1871, the German cannons were finally in place, and the shelling began. The guns boomed so loudly and so often that they created "one continuous noise," wrote a besieged city resident. Some four hundred shells fell on Paris each night. Throughout the city, people saw gaping holes in the sides of buildings and walls that had been riddled by bullets. The Parisians had guns and soldiers of their own, but their fighting force was smaller, and their weapons were inferior. By January 13, according to the official count, fifty-one residents of Paris had been killed, among them eighteen children.

At the Odéon, every day brought a fresh supply of wounded soldiers: fifty, a hundred, or more. Bernhardt threw all her energy into running the hospital. She hurried from one ward to another, dressing wounds, dispensing medicines, bathing patients, and offering comfort. She brought in her own stove and her personal cook to feed the

The Germans bombard Paris with their big guns.

men. When Paris ran out of firewood, she burned the theater's seats and scenery for warmth. She went without sleep, and often without food, and she grew thinner than ever before. The work exhausted her, but she never complained. As she did onstage, Bernhardt "took her role more than seriously and entered into the skin of her new character," observed Marie Colombier.

One night, some monks came to the hospital and asked for Bernhardt's help. There had been fighting; the monks hoped to borrow two carriages from her hospital to retrieve the casualties. Bernhardt did more than lend her carriages; she went with the monks. "Ah, what a horrible memory!" she said of that frigid, dark night. She and the monks listened for groans to guide them to the wounded. She came upon one man leaning against a heap of bodies. "I raised my lantern to look at his face and found that his ear and part of his jaw had been blown off," she wrote. "Great clots of blood, coagulated by the cold, hung from his lower jaw." Bernhardt had brought along a bottle of brandy. Using a piece of straw, she blew drops of the strong spirits into the man's torn mouth, hoping to give him strength. He was then lifted into one of the vehicles and transported to a hospital, possibly to die. Bernhardt wished she could have done more for him. "I sobbed at the thought of my helplessness," she said.

On January 27, after three weeks of shelling, France gave up. "Holding out was no longer possible," remarked the painter Édouard Manet, who had been in Paris throughout the hundred and thirty days that the Germans surrounded the city. "People were starving to death," he said. France and Prussia signed a peace agreement on the twenty-eighth. The conflict, remembered as the Franco-Prussian War, was over. As part of the accord, France ceded to Germany the eastern regions of Alsace and Lorraine. Despite its loss, the French government rewarded men and women who had displayed unusual patriotism and bravery. Among them was Sarah Bernhardt, who received a gold medal.

Her pride in being honored was swallowed up by "a terrible sadness," Bernhardt said. She was not alone in feeling this way. Sorrow at the defeat "took possession of everyone," she added, "even of the people who most ardently longed for peace." On February 17, the Germans staged a victory parade in Paris, a humiliation for the local people who had so bravely resisted the assault.

Throughout the siege, Bernhardt had heard nothing from her family. The Germans had severed Paris's telegraph lines. No letters could reach the city, and the only ones making it out were carried by pigeons or hot-air balloons. With the coming of peace, Sarah at last received a note from her mother. She learned that everyone was well—and staying in Germany, near the city of Frankfurt, where her aunt Rosine had friends. Sarah felt relieved and outraged at the same time. She was grateful to know that all were safe, but how dare her mother and aunts seek shelter in the land of France's enemy!

She was determined to get her family out of Germany, even if it meant crossing the former battle lines. The scene of the heaviest fighting was now a scarred landscape populated by gunmen, robbers, and looters. Sarah set out on a cold day with a young woman named Mademoiselle Soubise, who was Maurice's governess, and a hidden revolver. For the first part of the journey, the two women rode a train carrying German troops back to their homeland. There was no room for the women in the coaches, so they perched atop the coal that fed the engine, in an open car, exposed to the weather. An officer handed Bernhardt his warm coat, but she declined to take it. "I preferred dying of cold to muffling up in a cloak belonging to the enemy," she said.

When they could no longer go by train, Bernhardt and Soubise traveled by horse and cart. There were so many starts and stops that a trip expected to take three days lasted eleven. The women saw things they had hoped never to see: uprooted people wandering the roads and searching for lost relatives, and starving dogs tearing at the bodies of dead soldiers. At long last, they reached the house where Bernhardt's family was staying, and she held Maurice in her arms. "I found all my adored ones, big and little, and they were all very well. Oh, what happiness it was!" Sarah exclaimed. "I had suffered so much that I burst out into delicious laughter and sobs."

Getting back to Paris was easier, but Bernhardt and her family did not find a city at peace. Blaming the government for their defeat, many working-class Parisians had rebelled. They formed a radical socialist government of their own, which they called the Paris Commune. Looking out for the welfare of ordinary men and women, the Commune's leaders canceled people's debts and ended the obligation to pay rent. They took over hotels and vacant apartments to house people left homeless by the German guns. They emptied pawnshops and returned possessions to people who had sold them to buy food. They also banned night work for bakers, a move that made life easier for many workers. The "Communards" claimed to be carrying on "the struggle of the future against the past."

In March 1871, from Versailles, where the French government was temporarily headquartered, President Adolphe Thiers ordered the French army to descend on Paris and suppress the Commune. Gunfire broke out in the streets as the Communards, greatly outnumbered, defended their ideals fiercely. "No man of good sense could hope any longer for our victory," said one. Even children picked up weapons, fought, and died. Scenes of death and agony were everywhere. "There has been nothing but general butchery," noted the American minister to France. "The rage of the soldiers and the people knows no bounds." He mentioned "a well-dressed respectable looking man" who was "torn into a hundred pieces." His crime? "Expressing a word of sympathy for a man who was a prisoner and being beaten almost to death."

To escape the violence, Bernhardt moved to the suburb of Saint-Germain-en-Laye. There, from a high point, she watched flames rise from the great capital. The Communards had set fire to historic buildings such as Paris's city hall, the Hôtel de Ville. On May 24, flames gutted this stone structure and destroyed official documents stored in its offices, among them Sarah Bernhardt's birth certificate. The Commune executed prisoners loyal to the government, including the Archbishop of Paris. After a bloody week of fighting, government troops defeated the rebels. They, too, held executions, killing hundreds of Communards, male and female. They deported others to the French colony of New Caledonia, far off in the South Pacific.

Sarah Bernhardt understood the rage and suffering of Parisians who had survived the siege, but she hated the Commune and the destruction it had caused. Returning to Paris, she smelled "the bitter odour of smoke," she said, and looked around in disbelief. "What blood and ashes! What women in mourning! What ruins!" People cleared away the rubble and rebuilt damaged structures, and gradually

Parisians would rebuild the Hôtel de Ville in keeping with the original exterior design. The city government of Paris has been housed at this site since 1357.

the city returned to life. Within months, the Odéon was turned back into a theater, and Bernhardt received a notice to report for rehearsals. "I shook out my hair, stamped my feet, and sniffed the air like a young horse snorting," she said. She was eager and ready to get to work.

The Odéon was going to present *Ruy Blas,* the play it had withdrawn a few short years before at the government's request. Now Napoleon III was living in exile in England. The play's author, Victor Hugo, had returned to France after nineteen years on Guernsey. White haired and seventy years old, he was going to direct his own play, and Bernhardt was given a starring role. She was to portray a Spanish queen who falls in love with "Ruy Blas," a servant disguised as a nobleman.

Sarah Bernhardt had never met Victor Hugo, but she had been in

One of the world's great writers, Victor Hugo spent nearly two decades in exile after publicly denouncing Napoleon III.

awe of his greatness ever since reading his books as a schoolgirl. She pictured him as a severe, haughty man, almost a monster. This impression seemed to be confirmed when she was asked to report to his residence to read through the script. This was out of the ordinary, because actors almost always assembled in the theater for a first reading. Bernhardt asked herself, why should she, the star, cater to an old man's whims? She sent Hugo a note excusing herself because of illness. And when he replied with genuine concern about her health, she felt ashamed. Victor Hugo was kind, and she would soon discover that he was charming and witty as well. One day she saw him carry a sack of laundry across a busy boulevard for a poor old woman. "There was a moderation in his gestures, a gentleness in his way of speaking," she observed.

"Oh, those rehearsals of *Ruy Blas*!" she wrote in later life. "There was such good grace and charm about everything. When Victor Hugo arrived, everything brightened up."

Audiences loved the play, which opened in February 1872, and they would long remember Bernhardt as the queen. "All her movements are at once noble and harmonious," Parisians read in their newspapers. "Her voice is languishing and tender, her diction is of a rhythm so right

Bernhardt wowed audiences as the Spanish queen in *Ruy Blas*. Her performance earned her Victor Hugo's devotion.

and of a clarity so perfect that one never misses a syllable, even when the words leave her lips like nothing more than a caress." The critic even praised the folds of her silver gown, which arranged themselves around her body with perfect grace. After the final curtain fell on opening night, fans surrounded Bernhardt, offering their congratulations. The crowd parted to let Victor Hugo approach. He knelt before his star, took her hand, and kissed it.

FIVE

A Strange Girl in the Belle Époque

*She speaks entirely too fast, and this torrent is, in her,
a sign of inner emotion, which causes us to miss some of
her sentences. But her face is so expressive, all the passions are
painted there with such ferocious violence, that one reads on
her lively, expressive features the words that we do not hear.*
—Francisque Sarcey, theater critic

Peace settled on French shoulders like a fine velvet cloak. The tranquil decades that followed the Franco-Prussian War and Commune uprising came to be known as the *Belle Époque*. During these years, people devoted themselves to elegance and innovation. Impressionist painters used quick brushstrokes and bold colors to capture everyday life. French chefs perfected *haute cuisine*, taking cooking to a high level of refinement. Paris fashion houses elevated the art of draping the body. They produced chic dresses of satin and lace that were copied by dressmakers throughout Europe and America.

Thanks to the conveniences of modern life, many Europeans were enjoying something new called leisure time. They gathered in cafés to sip coffee and chat. Merrymakers flocked to cabarets like Paris's Moulin Rouge to see cancan dancers raise their skirts and kick up their

The Moulin Rouge, the most famous of Paris's cabarets, first opened its doors in 1889. Then, as now, it drew city residents and tourists out to have a good time.

legs. Of course, poverty dwelled in city slums and country villages. But hunger and hardship were easy to ignore so long as champagne flowed.

The theater remained as popular as ever, and Sarah Bernhardt was one of Paris's most admired performers. Her success in *Ruy Blas* brought a tempting offer from Émile Perrin, the new administrator of the Comédie-Française. The famed theater wanted her back, and Perrin promised to pay her well, despite the trouble she had caused there years before. Bernhardt had good reasons to say no. The stilted acting style preferred by the Comédie-Française restrained her natural impulses. Also, she was under contract with the Odéon for one more year. Bernhardt believed, though, that she had accomplished all she could at the Odéon, and she was ready for a change. She bought her way out of the contract for six thousand francs and prepared to take her chances.

On November 6, 1872, Sarah Bernhardt returned to the stage of the Comédie-Française. She starred in *Mademoiselle de Belle-Isle,* by Alexandre Dumas *père,* a drama of love and treachery set in the 1700s. The audience was mesmerized. One man compared her looks to portraits of saints painted by monks on medieval manuscript pages. She had "deep, shining, liquid eyes, a straight, fine nose," he wrote, and "red lips that open like a flower." He went on: her "heavy, enormous, abundant head of hair" was "very like the unruly tresses of goddesses." And her voice! It sounded like a song one of those goddesses might play on a lyre. In it he heard "the rhythm and music of poetry." In fact, "the higher the poetry rises, the more lyrical it grows, the loftier she becomes, the more she is herself."

The Comédie-Française cast Bernhardt in one play after another. She portrayed Grecian queens, Spanish noblewomen, and a wife

While some Parisians went to the theater and clapped for Sarah Bernhardt, others struggled to meet their basic needs. Poverty existed alongside gaiety in the years remembered as the Belle Époque. This woman looks after her children in the shabby Paris room that serves as the family's home.

betrayed by her husband. In *Rome vaincue,* she played an old blind woman, and viewers were in awe. "To simulate blindness, she contrives for half an hour at a time to show only the whites of her eyes"; this was "proof of her extraordinary intelligence and versatility," commented one theater critic. Because she often had to die tragically onstage, she visited hospitals and morgues to observe the dying and the dead. She used what she learned to make her death scenes seem authentic. For tourists in Paris, seeing Sarah Bernhardt onstage was as important as visiting Notre-Dame Cathedral or the Louvre.

All this effort took a toll. By 1874, Bernhardt was exhausted, and when she came down with a bad cough, she begged for a month off. Émile Perrin refused to give it to her, however. He insisted that she star in *Zaïre,* the play over which she had clashed with her teacher, Jean-Baptiste Provost.

Bernhardt was still sick on opening night, and she was furious with Perrin for ignoring her needs. It would serve him right, she told herself, if she really died onstage. With that thought in mind, her imagination went to work. "I gave myself entirely up to it," she wrote. When her character was stabbed, she convinced herself that she—Sarah Bernhardt—was in the final agonies of death. The scene felt so real that when the curtain fell, Bernhardt astonished herself by standing up and returning to life. It was a key moment in her development as an actor. "I learned that my vital forces were at the service of my mind," she noted, "having given out everything of which I was capable—and more." If she believed that what she was feeling was real, then the audience would believe it too. She was right; her fans loved her in *Zaïre.* Bernhardt would play the role many times throughout her career, always to acclaim.

Now sharing the stage with Bernhardt was Sophie Croizette, whom she had known in childhood, when they were both pupils at Notre-Dame du Grandchamp. Back then, Sophie was the prettier girl who won the best parts in school plays. She was still pretty and had grown into a curvy woman with blond hair and natural charm. Croizette and Bernhardt liked each other and were friendly rivals, each trying to win the choicest part and get top billing. Theatergoers had playful arguments about which woman they admired more: the soft, traditionally feminine Croizette or the elegant, eccentric Bernhardt. They divided themselves into two groups: the *Croizettistes* and the *Bernhardtistes*. "There were the stout bankers, the stout red-faced men, who enjoyed life, these formed the camp of Sophie Croizette," Bernhardt said. "Then there were the poets, the dreamers, the stu-

Sophie Croizette, Sarah Bernhardt's friendly rival, spent fourteen years with the Comédie-Française.

dents"—these, together with young girls, were Sarah Bernhardt's biggest fans.

Bernhardt performed as well with Jean Mounet-Sully, the leading male actor of the Comédie-Française. A solid figure with a booming voice and a large head of shaggy, dark curls, he was like a lion onstage. Bernhardt was small and delicate, yet she was strong enough to hold her own beside this roaring, gesturing man.

According to gossip printed in newspapers, Bernhardt and Mounet-Sully were carrying on a love affair offstage. The press linked Bernhardt romantically with many men: actors (especially her leading men), artists, Britain's Prince of Wales, and even the aged Victor Hugo. Often these reports were rumors and nothing more, but many of them were true, including this one. Bernhardt was involved with Mounet-Sully, who wrote poetry for her:

> *If we could love as the angels love;*
> *With a love so pure that the senses are banished . . .*

Before long, Bernhardt ended this romance because she and Mounet-Sully had little in common offstage, but they continued to act together.

Everything that Sarah Bernhardt did made news. The public read that she went horseback riding every day and that she kept a variety of pets. She had a parrot named Bizibouzon, a monkey named Darwin, and several dogs. Reporters described her unusual style of dress, how she draped herself in black lace, carried a thin walking stick, and wore a hat made from a stuffed bat.

At rehearsals, she put on a show of her own. "Unlike the other actresses, she comes all dressed up," playwright Octave Feuillet told his wife. "With her frizzy hair doing what it will and usually a few bunches of flowers in her fist, she goes through her role carefully and gravely as she should." At the end of rehearsals, she would do a little dance, jump off the stage, and sit at a piano, accompanying herself in song. Then she "starts to stride like a clown and crunches her chocolates, of which she keeps plenty in her pockets," Feuillet continued. "She takes out a little case that holds a lipstick, which she passes over her lips to redden them. She shows her teeth as white as fresh almonds and returns to crunching the chocolates." Feuillet could only remark, "What a strange girl."

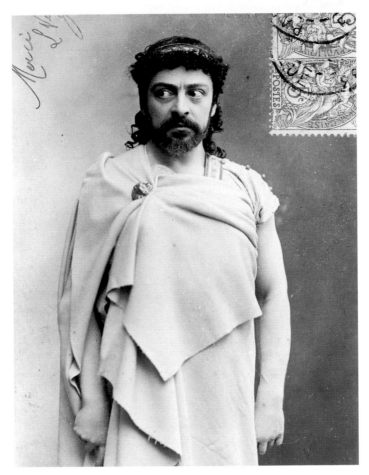

Jean Mounet-Sully was known for his arresting
appearance and energy onstage.

Bernhardt bought a coffin for her bedroom. She had herself photographed in it, dressed in white and covered with flowers. She claimed
that sleeping in the coffin reminded her of the mystery of death, but
the American writer Henry James thought he knew what she was up
to. "She has in a supreme degree what the French call the *génie de la
réclame*—the advertising genius," he observed. Bernhardt knew better
than anyone how to keep her face and name before the public.

She slept in the coffin while Régine spent the night in her bed.
Despite Sarah's love, Régine had grown up to be a troubled young
woman and a prostitute. At nineteen, she was dying. Tuberculosis was

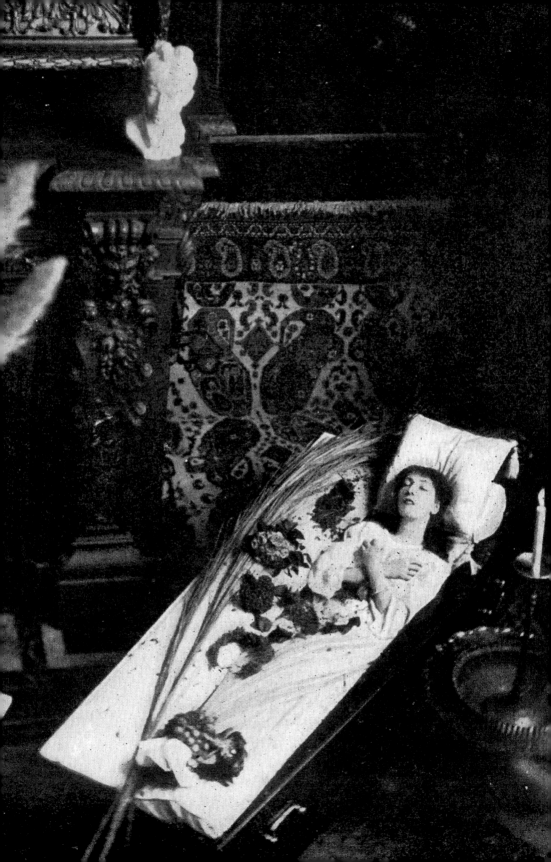

destroying her lungs and traveling through her bloodstream to damage other organs. Once a chubby, feisty girl, Régine had wasted away. She ran a constant fever, coughed up blood, and woke in the night drenched in sweat. There was nothing an older sister could do except make her comfortable and worry. There were no antibiotics; they would not be developed until the twentieth century. Régine Bernhardt died on December 16, 1873.

Sarah stood at the gates of Père Lachaise Cemetery on the day of Régine's funeral, with a black veil over her face. She suffered so visibly that some people accused her of staging a publicity stunt. "It's not a funeral, it's a première," was one journalist's unkind joke. Sarah Bernhardt's sorrow was no act, though. Her emotions overpowered her and made her ill, just as they had done when she was a child. This time Perrin needed no persuasion to give his star time off. Sarah went north to Brittany, the scene of her earliest memories. On a rocky beach, bracing herself against wintry sea winds, she watched waves crash against a lighthouse. Resting in this rugged place, she grew well again.

Once back in Paris, Bernhardt poured her energy into building a house, one free of painful reminders of Régine. It had a skylight and a large window to let in the sun, and scenes of life in China were painted on the entryway walls. She filled the rooms with tapestries, satin sofas, a jungle of tropical plants—and her many animals. A magazine writer who came calling remarked on her ten dogs: "These come in and out, examine you, take back their reports, return for further particulars, and at last range themselves in order of procession at your heels when you enter the drawing-room." He looked at the objects that furnished this chamber, dainty chairs and tall vases alongside easels, paintings in progress, and unfinished sculptures. He had to ask, "Is it a drawing-room or is it a studio?"

Sarah Bernhardt had herself photographed asleep in her coffin.

It was both. Many in Paris scoffed when Bernhardt announced that she was going to be an artist, but she ignored them and produced drawings, paintings, and figures in marble and bronze. The sculptor Auguste Rodin, creator of *The Thinker*, dismissed her work as rubbish and called the public stupid for giving it any attention. Some people whispered that other artists were putting the finishing touches on Sarah Bernhardt's creations. Nevertheless, she often had pieces accepted into the Paris Salon, the annual exhibition of new art that was judged to be the best in France. In 1876, she won a silver medal for *Après la tempête*, her statue of a woman of Brittany holding her drowned grandson after a storm.

Also in 1876, Sarah's mother, Youle Van Hard, died. "She was discovered one morning lying on her yellow sofa, dressed in a pretty négligé, with her head on a lace pillow," Sarah said. "Her beautiful hands held a tray-cloth which she had been embroidering. She was smiling, a coquette even in death." In her grief, Sarah took to her bed. Her mother had continually found fault with her and had rarely shown her kindness. Yet Sarah had always loved Youle and yearned to be close to her. She wept, knowing that now she and Youle would never have the close friendship that many mothers and their grown daughters enjoyed.

But life went on, and Sarah Bernhardt continued to act and make news. In the summer of 1878, she went often to the Exposition Universelle, the Paris world's fair. She loved to ascend in its hot-air balloon, which could not travel far, since a strong cable kept it tethered to the earth. Fifty people at once could rise above the fair in the balloon's enormous basket. They leaned over the edge to look down on the sights below, which included the head of Frédéric Auguste Bartholdi's *Liberty Enlightening the World*, known better as the *Statue of Liberty*. When completed, the statue would be a gift from France

For a European woman to wear pants in the nineteenth century was almost unheard of, but Bernhardt the artist selected them as her work clothes.

Bernhardt's prize-winning statue, *Après la tempête*, is now housed
in the National Museum of Women in the Arts, in Washington, D.C.

to the United States. Lifting their eyes, balloon riders gazed out over
the roofs and smokestacks of Paris to the suburbs and fields beyond.

Wanting a bigger thrill, Bernhardt talked Henri Giffard, the
engineer who had built the captive balloon, into sending her up
in one that flew freely through the air. One day before the summer
ended, a crowd gathered to watch Bernhardt step into the basket
attached to an orange hot-air balloon. She wore a feather-trimmed
jacket over her flowing dress and a pair of highly polished riding
boots. Her companion was an artist named Georges Clairin. He was
Bernhardt's current lover and would remain her lifelong friend. "Be
careful!" shouted Sarah's fans to the pilot, the third person aboard.
"Don't let her be killed!"

Up and away the balloon went, over houses, churches, and gardens, and over the stone pavement of streets and squares. Looking down on Père Lachaise Cemetery, Sarah dropped rose petals in memory of Régine and Youle.

Flying, she was entranced. She recited poetry as the balloon left foggy Paris behind; she and Clairin sang folksongs; they ate sandwiches of goose-liver *pâté* and drank champagne. The balloon rose higher, until it was a mile and a half above the earth. At that altitude, the thinning atmosphere gave Sarah a headache and made her nose bleed, so the pilot brought the craft down and landed it in a field.

The same day, Émile Perrin, director of the Comédie-Française, ran into an acquaintance on a Paris boulevard. This gentleman pointed toward the sky and said, "There goes your star." The next morning, furious that his most popular performer had foolishly put herself in danger, Perrin ordered Bernhardt into his office. Barely controlling his anger, he warned that he could fine her for breaking a rule of the Comédie-Française and leaving Paris without permission. Bernhardt shook her head. Pay a fine? Not likely! She offered to resign instead, forcing Perrin to withdraw his threat.

Unflustered, Bernhardt wrote a book about the balloon ride. *In the Clouds* tells the story of the flight from the point of view of a chair that was carried aloft for Bernhardt to use. The chair describes the sensations of flight. "I find a sky, blue, and a sun, radiant," it says. "Around and about us the cloud-mountains, opaque with rainbow-hued crests . . . It is astonishing! Not a sound, not even a whisper." The humble chair survives the flight and is brought to Bernhardt's home only to have a leg broken when it is accidentally dropped. Bernhardt repairs the chair, adorns it with medals, and places it among her treasured souvenirs. The chair is happy, having achieved all it ever dreamed of. This charming tale, illustrated by Clairin, became a bestseller.

Bernhardt, Georges Clairin, and a pilot sail through the sky in the basket of a hot-air balloon in this sketch by Clairin.

Soon Bernhardt was packing her bags for a different kind of travel. In June 1879, the Comédie-Française closed for six weeks for needed repairs to the theater. Perrin thought this was the ideal time for the actors to perform in London. The entire company rarely traveled outside France; for many British theatergoers, this chance to see the famed French troupe onstage would be a once-in-a-lifetime event.

Before she left, Bernhardt welcomed a visitor to her artist's studio. He was a silver-haired, neatly groomed Englishman named Edward Jarrett. He was an impresario, someone whose job it was to get theater bookings and publicity for people in show business. He promised to make money for Bernhardt by arranging for her to give private performances in the homes of London's wealthy. Perrin frowned on his actors performing on their own, but other members of the company would be doing it, although for less money than Bernhardt was to receive,

Jarrett said, if she employed his services. Bernhardt signed a contract with Jarrett, and he went to work.

Thanks to notices that Jarrett placed in British newspapers, most of the people who met the company's boat at Folkestone, England, had cheers and flowers for just one actor. "Vive Sarah Bernhardt!" they cried. "Hip, hip, hurrah!" A young Irish poet named Oscar Wilde dropped white lilies at her feet. And thanks to Jarrett's contacts in the press, Bernhardt spent her first day in London answering questions from reporters, with the impresario translating for her.

On opening night, knowing that many in the audience had come specially to see her, Bernhardt had a bad case of stage fright. She was starring as Phèdre, a Grecian queen who feels a forbidden love for her stepson and dies by swallowing poison. She fought to control her nerves as her admirers applauded her entrance on the stage. She made them a silent promise to do her best: "You shall see. I'm going to give you my very blood—my life itself—my soul." Then she started to speak, and her anxious voice sounded too high-pitched. Nevertheless, she drew on her inner resources. "I suffered, I wept, I implored, I cried out; and it was all real," she said. "My tears were flowing, scorching and bitter." It hardly mattered that Bernhardt and the other actors performed in French, a language only some in the audience understood. Many people referred to printed English translations to understand what was being said. For others, it was enough to absorb the emotions coming from the stage. In the final scene, Bernhardt fell into the arms of her costar and former lover, Mounet-Sully, who carried her drained body offstage. She was still leaning against him during the curtain calls, and the audience loved it.

In London, Bernhardt stayed in a luxurious house with fifteen-year-old Maurice, Georges Clairin, and Madame Guérard, whose children were now grown. She brought her many pets, and while in

Bernhardt and Mounet-Sully perform an emotional scene
during the Comédie-Française's London season.

England, she acquired more. From a supplier in Liverpool she bought a wolfhound, a cheetah, and several chameleons. The cheetah caused an uproar when Bernhardt released it in the backyard of her rented house. Her dogs barked in fright, Bizibouzon squawked in alarm, and the neighbors came running to see what was wrong. The chameleons fascinated Bernhardt with their ability to change color to match their surroundings. She placed a gold collar around the neck of one. It was attached to a chain that she pinned to her clothes so she could wear the little lizard like a piece of jewelry.

Dukes and duchesses and counts and countesses welcomed Bernhardt into their homes not only to perform but as a guest. This never happened in Paris, where the nobility knew all about the demimonde and had no wish to socialize with its inhabitants. Well-to-do Londoners were either ignorant of their city's shadowy side or pretended to one another that it did not exist. They were fascinated by Bernhardt with her open acknowledgment of her son born outside of marriage and unabashed sexual freedom. In London, Bernhardt was the latest novelty. When she held an exhibition of her art, four hundred people came to the opening, and her rich English fans bought most of the pieces.

The writer Henry James, then living in England, found it impossible to describe "the intensity, the ecstasy, the insanity as some people would say, of curiosity and enthusiasm provoked by Mlle. Bernhardt." Britain had never seen anyone like her. People praised her charm. They wondered at the despair she communicated when some of her lines were sighed rather than spoken. They loved the way she surprised them by being calm and controlled in one scene, only to explode in anguish or in rage the next. More than one person called her a genius. "She seemed like a leaf whirled away by the torrent of her passion," wrote one English theater critic.

Some people saw things differently. To them, her theatrics in London tarnished the dignity of the Comédie-Française. They pointed out that in an acting company, all the performers worked together to interpret a play. Giving too much attention to one belittled the contributions of others. Where was the praise, they asked, for Croizette, Mounet-Sully, and all the rest? In her own country, false rumors circulated about Bernhardt's activities offstage. People said that she was charging Londoners admission to see her in men's clothing, that she was smoking cigars and taking boxing lessons. They said vile things about her face, her thinness, and her Jewish heritage.

Bernhardt found hateful mail waiting for her when the Comédie-Française returned to Paris for the reopening of its theater. "My poor

Skeleton,—You will do well not to show your horrible Jewish nose at the opening ceremony," wrote one anonymous person. Her nose would make a perfect target, he warned, for the potatoes that Parisians were planning to throw at her.

SIX

WORLD-FAMOUS

I've seen Bernhardt!
Can one say more, except perhaps
to vainly rave, and feebly strive to tell
the world the joy
and rapture that she gave?
—Anonymous, "To Mme. Bernhardt"

Stay away from the theater, Émile Perrin advised Sarah. Give people time to forget the criticism you received in London. When the public is ready to welcome you back to the stage, well, you can appear then. Sarah disagreed. Her enemies might be vocal, but she would stand up to them. Besides, she had faith that her fans were loyal. She wanted to face them and affirm their affection and trust.

On the evening of the ceremony to reopen the theater, the actors stepped onstage in pairs, all except Sarah Bernhardt, who walked alone. "I strode to the footlights," she wrote. "I stood erect and gazed into the eyes turned toward me." There she waited, silent and vulnerable. She sensed a wave of emotion passing through the theater, touching one heart and then another. Was it love or hatred? Were these people friends who had come to welcome her, or foes waiting to boo her off the stage? She soon had her answer. "Suddenly the whole audience burst into a fanfare of bravos and applause," she noted. "It was one of the most beautiful moments of my career."

Once more, she was the toast of Paris. She electrified in *Ruy Blas* and other plays. At a banquet honoring Victor Hugo, she sat in a place of honor beside the great writer. Then, without warning, she resigned from the Comédie-Française. The theater company sued Bernhardt for breaking her contract and was awarded a hundred thousand francs in damages. She would pay this money gradually over the coming years.

While the case was in court, Bernhardt was back in London, performing with a new company of actors she had formed. She and her troupe were putting on modern plays, such as *Froufrou*, which is about a foolish young wife who embarks on a love affair. Sorry for what she has done, the wife begs her husband's forgiveness, swallows poison, and dies.

Another play, *Adrienne Lecouvreur,* was just as melodramatic. It was based on the true story of an eighteenth-century stage star who died after sniffing poisoned violets. "Never has an audience been so moved," stated a Frenchman in London who saw it. As Adrienne Lecouvreur, Bernhardt "rose to a dramatic power, a level of truth, that can never have been surpassed." He wished a French audience had heard her cry out, "I do not want to die!" They would have "burst into sobs and ovations," the Frenchman believed.

Sarah Bernhardt and her company acted for audiences throughout France and in other European countries. The hurrah that greeted Bernhardt's train when it pulled into Copenhagen was so thunderous that it frightened her. Two thousand people stood along the streets of that city to cheer and throw flowers as she headed toward her hotel. The Danish royal family came to see her perform, and King Christian IX gave her an honorary medal. He allowed her to use the royal yacht

Sarah Bernhardt in *Froufrou*. For much of her life, Bernhardt was considered unusually thin. Critics compared her body to a billiard cue, a corkscrew, or a snake. Bernhardt's weight would appear normal today, but at the time, a full, round figure was the standard of beauty.

for a jaunt to Kronborg Castle, near the town of Elsinore, the setting of Shakespeare's *Hamlet*.

While in Denmark, Bernhardt attended a dinner held in her honor. Among the guests was Baron Magnus, the Prussian ambassador, who stood to make a toast. "I drink to France, which has given us such great artists," he said, raising his glass. Sarah was taken aback. The German states had defeated France ten years before. They had snatched up Alsace and Lorraine, which the French considered their own. Now the ambassador was toasting France as though the two nations were old friends. Needing to speak up for her country, Sarah Bernhardt rose and faced the baron. "Yes, let us drink to France," she concurred. "But to the whole of France, Your Excellency."

Bernhardt was working harder than ever, but she never fell sick from overwork as she had in the past. She credited her good health to being her own boss. It was she who decided which plays to perform, where, and when. She chose her costumes and costars. As she put it, "The ability to do as I wanted without interference and out of anyone's control calmed my nerves." She slept better at night, ate healthier meals, and felt restored.

Edward Jarrett, the impresario, was setting up something grander for Sarah Bernhardt: an American tour. She would be away from France for seven months, and she would return a wealthy woman. Jarrett had arranged for her to receive five hundred dollars for each performance in the United States and Canada. (Five hundred U.S. dollars in 1880 had the buying power of roughly $11,500 in 2018.) In New York City alone, she was scheduled to appear twenty-seven times. Also, if a theater took in more than three thousand dollars for one evening, then Bernhardt was to receive half of anything over that amount. All this was in addition to what she earned from sales of her paintings and sculpture. Exhibitions were being planned for New York and Boston.

The adventure began in mid-October 1880, when Bernhardt sailed for New York on an old steamship called the *Amérique*. The hardest part of leaving was saying goodbye to Maurice. He sometimes traveled with Bernhardt in the summer, but at other times he had to go to school. He was staying with her aunt Henriette and uncle Félix, and Bernhardt knew he would be safe. She felt happy knowing that Madame Guérard, her little lady, would be with her while she was away. Her current lover, an actor named Édouard Angelo, was also at her side. He would play the leading male roles in the dramas that she performed. And she

Bernhardt hired Marie Colombier, who had attended the Conservatoire with her and worked in her wartime hospital, to perform on the American tour.

brought one dog, a Brussels griffon named Hamlet. Her sister, Jeanne, was supposed to come as well. Sarah was trying to help Jeanne, who was addicted to morphine, although Sarah often had no idea whom Jeanne was seeing or what she was doing. When it was almost time to sail, an overdose landed Jeanne in a hospital. So Sarah invited Marie Colombier, her friend from the Conservatoire, to take her sister's place. Colombier, who was in debt, welcomed this chance to put many miles between herself and her creditors. Jeanne would cross the Atlantic and catch up with the troupe when she had recovered.

The eleven-day voyage to New York was exciting—as Bernhardt described it in her memoirs. She claimed, for example, that she saved the life of Mary Todd Lincoln, who was on the same ship, sailing home from a European vacation. Bernhardt told readers that the widow of President Abraham Lincoln was strolling on deck one cold morning when a large swell crashed against the ship and sent her tumbling. Bernhardt, who was out walking too, grabbed a bench and steadied herself. With her free hand, she caught Mrs. Lincoln's black skirt just as that lady was about to fall down a flight of stairs. "Very much hurt though she was, and a trifle confused, she thanked me in such a gentle dreamy voice that my heart began to beat with emotion," Bernhardt wrote.

A few days later, the ship's doctor led her to the steerage, the section where the poorest passengers rode. Many of these people were leaving Europe behind to take their chances in the New World. An emigrant woman was giving birth, and the doctor brought Bernhardt to help. "I went at once to the mother, and did all I could for the poor little creature who had just come into the world," Bernhardt wrote. The doctor handed her the newborn and asked her to bathe him in a basin. Bernhardt remarked on the tiny boy's strength and determination: "Oh, that first strident cry of the child affirming its will to live in the midst of all these sufferings, of all these hardships, and of all these hopes!" The proud mother and father asked Bernhardt to be baby Robert's godmother.

The *Amérique* docked in New York City early on the cold, sunny morning of October 27. Thousands of people swarmed the pier, eager to see the "Divine Sarah," as she was called. City officials rushed to greet her as a band struck up "La Marseillaise." Bernhardt would hear the French national anthem often in her travels. Gliding "as lightly and as rapidly as a leaf borne along by the wind," the famous star was an "apparition," a newspaper told its readers. "Mlle. Bernhardt is a lady of middle height, erect in carriage, and of a girlish, not angular physique. A perfect head, set almost defiantly on a slim and delicate neck, is crowned by a wealth of silken hair with a tint of burnished gold." When she passed through customs, an officer searching her velvet handbag saw that she had brought Maurice's baby shoes to remind her of her son and her love for him.

New York, a bustling commercial and cultural center, welcomed Sarah Bernhardt.

Americans wanted to know everything about the legendary actor. They had heard about her illegitimate son. They had read that her lovers included the tsar of Russia and the pope. Reporters crowded around, asking foolish questions: Was it true that she smoked cigars? Did she really feed live quails to her lions? What was her favorite food? Bernhardt confirmed what was true, denied the wild rumors, and said that she liked mussels. To see her onstage at the Booth Theatre, New Yorkers stood in a line stretching several city blocks. They paid as much as sixty dollars for a single ticket, an unheard-of amount in the nineteenth century.

They got their money's worth. Bernhardt and her troupe presented such crowd pleasers as *Adrienne Lecouvreur,* about the actor who dies after smelling flowers, and *Phèdre,* in which the Grecian queen poisons herself. They introduced new plays that soon became audience favorites. One was *La Dame aux camélias*. (The title means The Lady with Camellias; in the United States this play was often called *Camille*, although no character has this name.) In this tragic drama by Alexandre Dumas *fils* (son, or junior), Bernhardt portrayed a courtesan who falls in love only to die of tuberculosis. "I am dying, but I am happy, and my happiness hides my death," she says in her final moments. Bernhardt's sensational death scenes earned her standing ovations and many curtain calls. American theatergoers had rarely seen such a polished, elegant performer. When she was not onstage, fans gathered outside her hotel to cheer and serenade her. They waited for their idol to step out on her balcony and blow kisses their way.

While in New York, Bernhardt saw a play featuring Clara Morris, a popular American star. Morris acted in overly emotional dramas and had a talent for crying buckets of tears. The audience applauded Bernhardt as she took her seat, and she graciously waved. When Clara Morris stepped in front of the closed curtains, Bernhardt took off the corsage of white roses that she wore and tossed it to the American as an offering of friendship. Blunt-speaking Marie Colombier, who sat with Bernhardt that night, passed judgment, declaring that Morris "had never possessed beauty. In her youth, perhaps, but that was long ago." Her mouth was "a black hole. Her teeth resembled cloves stuck in sealing wax." This was a mean thing to say, but it was true. A theater critic commenting on Morris said, "She would appear young enough if it was not for her teeth, which are ragged and black, and which she seems to purposely expose on all occasions, rather than hide."

From New York, the actors traveled to Boston, the next city on the tour. On the way, their train made a nighttime stop in Menlo Park, New Jersey, so Bernhardt could meet Thomas Edison. A carriage brought her through a snow-covered landscape to the famed inventor's home. Wrapped in fur, Bernhardt felt drowsy until the trees and bushes around her suddenly glowed with light. How

Clara Morris (seated, in a blond wig) was a popular American actor.

marvelous! In 1879, Edison had created the first incandescent lightbulb that could be manufactured and sold in stores to people wanting to illuminate their houses with electricity. He was using those bulbs to light up his grounds at night. Electric streetlights had been installed in Paris in 1878, but Parisians relied on oil and gas lamps in their homes. Electric lamps would not come into Paris houses until 1888.

Bernhardt spotted Thomas Edison and his family standing on their porch. Edison had "wonderful blue eyes, more luminous than his incandescent lamps," Bernhardt observed. His large head and noble profile reminded her of portraits of Napoleon Bonaparte. Bernhardt sensed that the thought of entertaining a celebrity bored Edison, so she turned on all her charm and tried not to ask foolish questions. "I made such an effort, and succeeded so well that half an hour later we were the best of friends," Bernhardt wrote.

Edison led his guest up narrow stairs and across bridges suspended high over furnaces to give her a tour of his laboratory. "The deafening sound of the machinery, the dazzling rapidity of the changes of light, all that together made my head whirl," Bernhardt stated. Once her dizziness passed, Edison demonstrated his recent inventions for her, including the phonograph. He even recorded her reciting verses from *Phèdre*. She joined the Edisons for a late dinner and climbed back into her carriage in the wee hours of the morning.

Bernhardt and her company next went to the Canadian city of Montreal, where many residents spoke French. Again, thousands turned out to welcome her. People shouted, *Vive Sarah Bernhardt! Vive la France!* Local church leaders were not quite so thrilled. The Roman Catholic bishop ordered the faithful to stay away from Bernhardt's shows. She was an immoral woman, just like the adulterous wives and courtesans she played onstage, he said. What was more, she would be performing on Christmas, one of the holiest days of the year.

Thomas Edison welcomed Sarah Bernhardt into the Menlo Park, New Jersey, laboratory where he had worked on electric lighting, the phonograph, and other inventions.

Most people ignored the bishop's command. The mayor of Montreal saw Bernhardt in a play, and so did judges and members of Quebec's parliament. "Both English and French speaking Montreal were there in all their splendour," wrote one reporter. After a performance of *Adrienne Lecouvreur*, her adoring fans unhitched the horses from her carriage and hauled it themselves through the cold streets to return her to her hotel.

Sarah Bernhardt played in Detroit, Cincinnati, Toronto, Atlanta, Memphis, Washington, D.C.—fifty-one places in all. At every stop, crowds greeted the famous French actor. Thanks to Edward Jarrett's advance publicity, nearly every person in the United States had heard about Bernhardt's tour. An American newspaper, the *Connecticut Courant,* called her "the most extensively advertised woman the world ever saw." Outside theaters, fans shoved to get near her to beg for an autograph or simply to touch her fur coat. One rabid admirer snipped a feather off her hat.

She went from town to town in style, in a private railroad car that was like a traveling hotel. It featured a parlor decorated with plush furniture, stained-glass windows, brass lamps, and a piano. A woodburning stove provided constant warmth. A separate dining car held a table for ten, with linens, plates, and utensils all marked with Bernhardt's motto, *Quand Même.* Two cooks prepared meals in the car's kitchen. There was a bedroom for Bernhardt and Édouard Angelo, where Hamlet, the little dog, slept in a beribboned basket. According to Marie Colombier, Bernhardt acquired another animal in New Orleans, an alligator named Ali-Gaga. It went with Bernhardt everywhere, drawing frightened stares from the public. Bernhardt and her friends fed Ali-Gaga milk and champagne, a diet that was ultimately fatal to the alligator.

There were feats of daring and close calls along the way. Upon leaving New Orleans, Bernhardt was informed that a nearby railroad bridge had been weakened by floodwaters and declared unsafe. It was possible to avoid it, but that meant following a longer route and falling behind schedule. Willing to take a risk rather than lose time, Bernhardt gave the wary engineer twenty-five hundred dollars to take her company across. The frightened passengers held their breath as the train thundered over the bridge. Madame Guérard blessed herself again and again. Edward Jarrett nervously chewed a cigar. Marie Colombier clutched little Hamlet while Sarah hugged her sister Jeanne.

She offered a silent plea to Mother Sainte Sophie, the beloved director of her old school. She hoped the gentle nun was watching from heaven.

Moments after the train was across, the bridge collapsed with a deafening crash. Crew and passengers were safe, but the reality of the danger they had faced sank in. Bernhardt shuddered to think of the lives she had put in peril merely to save several hours. "My conscience was by no means tranquil, and for a long time my sleep was disturbed by the most frightful nightmares," she confessed. "And when any of the artistes spoke to me of their child, their mother, or their husband, whom they longed to see once more, I felt myself turn pale."

The American tour ended in New York City, where it had begun, with a performance of *La Dame aux camélias* on May 3, 1881. Bernhardt had been onstage in America one hundred and fifty-six times and was taking home $194,000. She was thirty-six years old and had been adored like no star before her. "Come back, Sarah! Come back!" people cried. She would come back—seven times, in fact.

Sarah Bernhardt's homecoming was joyous. Among the friends and admirers waiting to greet her at Le Havre was Maurice, who had grown in seven months as only a teenage boy can do. He was noticeably taller and starting to look more like a young man, and he made his mother proud. The fishermen of Le Havre presented her with a bouquet of flowers. They asked Bernhardt if she and the actors would put on a play to benefit the families of local men lost at sea. She agreed to do it without hesitation.

She and her actors next spent six months performing throughout Europe. In Russia they gave a command performance for Tsar Alexander III and Empress Maria Feodorovna at the Winter Palace in Saint Petersburg. Every nation she visited honored Bernhardt as a great artist. She received a diamond brooch from the king of Spain and a cameo necklace from the emperor of Austria.

At some time during the European tour, Sarah Bernhardt met Ambroise Aristide Damala. Handsome, with dark hair and eyes, Jacques Damala, as he was called, had been born into a family of Greek aristocrats and raised in France. He was a thrill seeker who had served in Africa with the Foreign Legion, a branch of the French army formed to protect France's colonies in other parts of the world. He had inherited wealth when his father died but had spent most of it on lavish parties for his friends. Now he aspired to be an actor, although he had no training or experience.

And Sarah Bernhardt fell in love with him. What was more, "I made up my mind to marry him," she said. On April 4, 1882, during a brief trip to London, she did.

Sarah Bernhardt watched her son grow up quickly.

SEVEN

PUBLIC WOMAN/ PRIVATE LIFE

Sarah Bernhardt has taken a master
She has lost her liberty
Sarah Bernhardt has just committed
her latest eccentricity.
—Anonymous, "Le Mariage de Sarah Bernhardt"

ad Sarah Bernhardt lost her good sense along with her heart? Maurice hated her new husband, and so did others. "Damala was the most cold-blooded, cynical, and worthless individual whom I had ever met. I could not bear the sight of him," commented Sarah's friend Thérèse Berton, an actor's wife. Someone else wrote, "I am acquainted with many personal friends of Sarah Bernhardt . . . Among them all, I have not found two who anticipate that the happy couple will long dwell together in unity." The friends counted the reasons this marriage was doomed. Jacques was full of himself—that was one. They had heard him insult Sarah in public—that was another. He was spending her money (which, as her husband, he was entitled by law to do). But he was buying gifts for other women and morphine for himself.

Yes, Jacques Damala was addicted to drugs. "He looked like a dead man," observed the Irish writer Bram Stoker, who dined with Bernhardt and Damala one night. "I sat next to him at supper, and the idea that he was dead was strong on me. I think he had taken some mighty dose of opium, for he moved and spoke like a man in a dream. His eyes, staring out of his white, waxen face, seemed hardly the eyes of the living." Stoker would recall Damala's corpse-like face several years later, when creating his most famous character, Count Dracula.

At the same dinner, Bernhardt was "charming and fresh and natural," Stoker wrote. "Every good and fine instinct of her nature seemed to be at the full when she was amongst artistic comrades whom she liked and admired. She inspired every one else and seemed to shed a sort of intellectual sunshine around her."

Either Sarah was blind to Jacques's faults or she overlooked them as she poured her energy into his acting career. On May 26, 1882, the newlyweds appeared together in Paris, in *La Dame aux camélias*. Curious people flocked to the theater to get a look at Sarah Bernhardt's husband and watch her act out love scenes with him. "Damala! There he is. Ah! Ah! Ah!" audience members exclaimed in loud whispers as he made his entrance. They fixed their opera glasses on the young man with short hair and a pointed beard, and they admired his looks if not his talent. "His inexperience is colossal; his voice is low and all but inaudible; his diction is sloppy," lamented a theater critic. "In brief, it was not a happy display."

Sarah, undaunted, worked with her husband to improve his acting. She rented a Paris theater and had a play written for him. Titled *Les Mères ennemies*, this play concerns a man and two women—his current and former wives—who are the enemies of the title. Sarah gave her

Jacques Damala in costume for a stage role.

son, Maurice, the double duties of managing the theater and directing the play. Maurice was eighteen, and Sarah was helping launch his
career too. Both men were novices, and neither felt friendly toward
the other. Nevertheless, *Les Mères ennemies* opened in mid-November
to fair reviews.

Sarah Bernhardt, meanwhile, appeared in a different theater, in
another new play. In *Fédora,* she portrayed a Russian princess who
tries to avenge the slaying of her fiancé. The princess's efforts go
wrong and cause two innocent people to die. She then takes poison
and, predictably, dies. The playwright, Victorien Sardou, had written *Fédora* with Bernhardt in mind, and it was a huge hit. "The great

Sarah!" raved one person who saw the play. "She was wonderful in her catlike grace and in her fury! She tossed out her words with a brusque simplicity that made all the audience shudder!" *Fédora* became one of Bernhardt's most popular plays. She would star in it many times in the years to come.

Her success made Damala furious. How dare his wife steal attention away from him? He would show her; he would show the whole nation. He announced in February 1883 that he was giving up acting and going back to the French Foreign Legion. "France, which treats my wife as a spoiled child, will, I hope, have room for me under the shadow of her flag," he declared. Away he went, forcing his play to close. For Sarah, there was no time to weep. Rent was due on the theater, and she needed money to pay it. Jacques had spent so much of her wealth that she had no choice but to sell her jewelry. Pearls, diamonds, sapphires, and rubies, many of them gifts from royalty, all had to go. Sarah sold them without regret. She had bounced back before, and she would do so again. *Quand même.*

To earn some of what she had lost, she went on the road, performing in *Fédora* throughout Europe. She returned home to find that Damala had come back to Paris. He was living in her house, falling in and out of consciousness, weak and ill from morphine abuse. Sarah no longer believed that she could live happily with Jacques, or that he could succeed as an actor. It was time to face reality. Wanting to do what was best for them both, Sarah paid for Jacques to go to a sanitarium and hoped that he could overcome his addiction. As for herself, "My husband had spurned the affection and love which I had lavished upon him," she said. "And now I wanted to recover from that love."

She had barely restored her spirit when, in December, her friend Marie Colombier published a scandalous book. Still trying to get out of debt, Colombier had turned to writing to make money. *The Memoirs of Sarah Barnum* was a novel, but the story it told was a thinly disguised account of Sarah Bernhardt's life. Its tone was mocking, and its content was anti-Semitic. Its heroine, Colombier wrote, was a "miserly Jewess." It made terrible claims, alleging, for example, that when Sarah was young, her godfather sexually abused her, with her mother's encouragement. Colombier also stated that "Sarah Barnum" hated her little sister and had pushed her into prostitution. The false accusation hurt, because Sarah believed she had done her best for Régine. The younger girl had lacked Sarah's inner strength and never rose above their mother's rejection. The pain it caused had led Régine into a self-destructive life. Questions raced through Bernhardt's mind. Why had Marie published such a nasty book? Was she jealous of Sarah's success? Was she exploiting her friend's fame for profit? And should she get away with it?

Maurice Bernhardt thought not. One afternoon, he showed up uninvited at Colombier's apartment. "Madame," he said, "if you have a gentleman friend who will come to your defense, I am ready to fight him in a duel." Maurice had been taught to handle a sword. His mother had raised him to fit in with the upper crust of society, for whom fencing was a popular sport. But Colombier saw before her an inexperienced youth and was unimpressed. She rejected his challenge and replied, "If I have a quarrel with Mademoiselle Sarah Bernhardt, let her address me, one woman to another." Maurice, deflated, turned around and left.

Minutes later, Sarah herself burst into Colombier's home, brandishing a horsewhip. She charged through the rooms, lashing furniture, figurines, vases—destroying anything within reach. According to Sarah, she whipped Marie, too, cutting her face and forcing her to flee down a back stairway. Colombier told a different story, that she hid behind a curtain and watched the assault on her belongings without being touched.

Newspapers in Paris and beyond reported on the strange escapade. Many declared that Bernhardt had acted foolishly. "Sarah Bernhardt would have done better to stay at home, wrapped in her dignity as a great artist, and let public disdain do justice to that abominable book" was the common opinion. What happened next was ironic. Before Bernhardt descended on Colombier's home, very few copies of the book had been sold. After the whip attack made news, the novel flew off bookstore shelves. The publisher planned a second, larger printing, and orders poured in from Germany, Italy, and Russia. Marie Colombier earned a handsome profit, more than enough to replace her damaged furnishings. "And who created all this publicity around the scandal?" asked one commentator. "The defamed one, the victim."

At least Sarah could count on the public to love her. In the decades to come, she lived a rambling life, alternating seasons in Paris and London with performing tours in other parts of the world. In 1886 she embarked on a thirteen-month trip to South, Central, and North America. She performed her most popular roles, won over new fans, and was treated like visiting royalty. The government of Argentina deeded her thirteen thousand acres, which she never saw and had no clue how to locate. In Ecuador a naval officer gave her a tiger cub, which caused trouble later in Chicago, when it bit a waiter's arm. In Chile the poet Rubén Darío went into raptures after seeing her in *Fédora*. "She is the drama, body and soul. Her beautiful form stands out like a magical apparition," he wrote. "She is unconquerable, the passion that moans and stirs. She is the absolute queen of art in its highest form: real life."

With the money she earned on tour, Bernhardt moved to a grander house on Paris's boulevard Pereire, a street that was home to artists, composers, and writers. The centerpiece of this dwelling was a two-story salon with a glass roof. Bernhardt filled it with her satin-covered furniture, pillows, and animal skins. On its red walls she hung mementoes of her travel, everything from Mexican daggers to Italian gilded mirrors. Bernhardt would live here for the rest of her life.

She also bought another house not far from her own—as a wedding

Sarah Bernhardt photographed in her sumptuously decorated home.

present. On December 28, 1887, Maurice, now twenty-three, married a young woman from a Polish noble family. Maria Teresa Jablonowska went by the nickname Terka. When Bernhardt was in Paris, the newlyweds often joined her for Sunday dinner. Family gatherings were especially joyful after the couple's first child, a girl named Simone, was born, in 1889. Sarah, at forty-four, liked to call herself "the youngest grandmother in France."

Sarah Bernhardt knew all too well that when life seemed sweetest, sorrow might soon be upon her. In summer 1889, word came that Jacques Damala was near death. Immediately, Sarah forgot his shameful treatment of her. She rushed to his address and found him in a filthy, rundown room, his body and mind ravaged by morphine and cocaine. There was only one thing for her to do: she had him moved to her home and nursed him round-the-clock. For a while he seemed to improve, until one day he lost consciousness and fell to the floor. He was taken to a hospital, where, on August 18, he died. Sarah wore her wedding ring for a long time to come, and she signed her letters "the widow Damala." Her husband had been a flawed, disturbed man. Despite her brave words when they separated, she had never stopped loving him.

Travel offered distraction, and Bernhardt liked seeing new places. In 1891, she left on a long overseas tour. She made news when she reached Australia and authorities seized the two dogs she had brought along for company. Concerned that foreign dogs might bring rabies into the country, the Australian government required them to be quarantined for six months. If they remained free of disease, they could join their owner at the end of that period. Bernhardt could not bear to think of her cherished pets locked up and feeling abandoned. She issued an appeal for help, and, luckily, a fellow French citizen kindly offered them a temporary home.

The scientist Adrien Loir lived and worked on Rodd Island, in Sydney's Parramatta River. He had come to Australia to help that nation solve its rabbit problem. Back in 1859, a hunter had released two dozen rabbits in the Australian wild. With no natural enemies on the continent, the rabbits had multiplied at an astounding rate. Soon they were devouring crops and livestock feed. By the 1880s, Australians were capturing and killing millions of rabbits, but many more were born to replace them. Loir believed that he could control the rabbits by infecting them with chicken cholera, a disease that was lethal to poultry. He was testing his idea in his laboratory, at a safe distance from the mainland. Responding to Bernhardt's plea, he persuaded government officials to declare the island an official quarantine site, and the dogs were allowed to stay there. The actor could visit whenever she liked.

What a relief! While she was performing in Australia, Bernhardt saw her dogs every weekend (and drank champagne on the laboratory roof with Adrien Loir). She bought another dog, a Saint Bernard. Because he was born in Australia, he was welcome wherever Bernhardt went. He drank water from a silver bowl in her flower-filled hotel suite and escorted her to the theater each evening. She trained him to kiss her other new animals: an Australian opossum that nibbled on roses and a koala that napped in the cover of a traveling case. As for the scientist, Adrien Loir, he had hoped that infected rabbits would transmit chicken cholera to others in the wild, but they did not. His experiment a failure, he returned to France. To this day, rabbits continue to take an environmental toll in Australia.

In Sydney as everywhere, people wanted to know what Sarah Bernhardt was like. Her "strong personality is one of her most powerful charms," they read in the *Sydney Mail*. "Her welcome is hearty; she speaks warmly and gracefully." Portraits failed to give a true impression of her, wrote the reporter who interviewed Bernhardt. He remarked on her eyes, which were "a deep grey-violet veiled with long lashes; the eyebrows full and well marked, a classic nose, very mobile mouth, and well-formed chin." That chin, he noted, was half hidden in her feathery collar. Her once-golden hair was now dyed a "deep Titian red."

When she was not on tour, Bernhardt produced, directed, and starred in plays at Paris's Théâtre de la Renaissance, which she leased. There, in the 1890s, she presented plays that became standards in her repertoire. She starred as Cleopatra and used a live snake for the death scene, in which the Egyptian queen is bitten by an asp. She portrayed Joan of Arc, the fifteenth-century country girl who fought for France against England in the Hundred Years War. Joan, who wore men's clothing, was burned at the stake for the crime of heresy when she was only nineteen. Bernhardt was much older, but she summoned the feelings and movements of youth.

Bernhardt as a bejeweled Cleopatra.

In *Théodora*, by Victorien Sardou, Bernhardt portrayed another historical figure, a Byzantine empress. The real Théodora died of cancer, but in Sardou's play, she is handed over to an executioner, which made for sensational drama. Bernhardt adored acting in *Théodora*. As a play, it was "superb, simply superb," she said. In Sardou's *La Tosca*, she took the part of Floria Tosca, an Italian opera star. Tosca murders Scarpia, Rome's chief of police, while attempting to save her lover, waits execution in prinson. The plan fails, and Tosca takes her own life by jumping from a high wall. Bernhardt held the audience rapt as she stealthily grasped a dagger and plunged it into Scarpia's flesh. People held their breath as she placed two candles on the floor beside the dead man and a crucifix on his chest. Their eyes never left her as she slinked from the room to her gruesome death. The Italian composer Giacomo Puccini was so taken with *La Tosca* that he wrote an opera based on Sardou's play. The sopranos of that time studied Bernhardt's performance, especially the murder scene, and tried to play the role in the same transfixing way.

In August 1894, when many Parisians went on vacation, Sarah Bernhardt returned to the Brittany seashore. One day, she took a steamboat out to a small, windswept island known as Belle-Île. She fell in love with the island's steep hills and its wildflowers struggling to grow. Standing on its rocky coast and looking out at the rolling ocean, she felt renewed. At the northwest tip of the island, she came upon a small fort. It was old, abandoned, and buffeted by winds, and it was for sale. Looking at the fort, Sarah saw what it could become: a summer house to share with her family and friends, far from reporters and curious fans. She bought the old place from the French government and turned it into the home she envisioned. Workers created an art studio, a tennis court, and ample guest quarters.

For years to come, she spent happy, relaxed summers on Belle-Île. On some clear mornings, after a seaweed bath (which she believed was good for her health), Sarah sunbathed, in a manner of speaking. She sat in the sun but protected her skin with a Japanese robe, a panama hat, and a green veil that wrapped around her neck. On other days, she donned her bathing costume, with its long skirt, silk stockings, and shoes, and waded into the sea to catch prawns that flitted among the rocks. After lunch and a nap, she and her visitors admired her flowers, rode horses, or played tennis. "It is not easy to play tennis with Sarah," confessed the composer Reynaldo Hahn, a frequent guest at Belle-Île. Jumping from a rooftop as Floria Tosca night after night onstage had

Having murdered the police chief, Scarpia, Bernhardt's character
prepares to place candles beside his body in *La Tosca*.

damaged her right knee, making it painful for her to run and lunge.
She expected tennis opponents to aim the ball to the spot where
she stood.

Dinner in the fort was the time for lively, noisy talk. After the meal,
one friend might go to the piano and pound out a tune. Others would
then get up from the table and dance, while Bernhardt watched their

Sarah Bernhardt
is dressed for
tennis. An ample
scarf holds her
hat in place and
protects her from
the sun.

Bernhardt's fortress home on Belle-Île nestles in the rugged landscape that she loved.

fandangos, reels, and dizzying twirls. Pretty soon, even the lamps would shake. "We give ourselves over to wild hilarity, laughing until it hurts," Hahn wrote. "Sarah, her head in her hands, laughs until she is hiccupping and sobbing. She pauses to catch her breath and sits back with her eyes closed, only to lean forward and start laughing again."

At Belle-Île, Sarah Bernhardt "was irresistibly comic at times, full of bubbling gaiety and spirits," remarked another guest. "What struck me most about her, when I saw her in private life, was her radiant and ever-present common-sense. There was no nonsense about her, no pose, and no posturing. She was completely natural."

The Great and Good Sarah

You know well, Sarah, that sometimes
You feel, while playing a role, the secret touch
Of Shakespeare's lips upon your jeweled fingers.
—Edmond Rostand, dramatist and poet

On the gray morning of January 5, 1895, a crowd formed outside the iron fence surrounding the École Militaire, France's national war college. A somber ceremony was about to begin. Captain Alfred Dreyfus of the French army was to be stripped of his rank in partial punishment for the crime of espionage.

An order was issued, and the prisoner was led to the center of the college courtyard. The onlookers saw a slender man with a dignified bearing and gentle eyes behind wire-rimmed glasses. They saw a sergeant step forward and rip the insignia, buttons, and trouser stripes from Dreyfus's uniform. The sergeant took Dreyfus's sword, held it over his own knee, and broke it in half. "In the name of the people of France, we degrade you," said the general in charge, who was on horseback.

Dreyfus spoke up, addressing everyone present. "They are degrading an innocent man," he said. "Long live France! Long live the Army!" The crowd responded with a chant: "Death to the Jew!"

Dreyfus, who was Jewish, had not been condemned to death, but some said his sentence was worse. He was to spend the rest of his life behind bars in the infamous prison colony on Devil's Island. Located off the coast of South America, Devil's Island was a dreadful place. Its prisoners often died violently, at the hands of guards or other inmates, or succumbed to starvation or tropical diseases. Quite a few went mad. "Here are Men in Hell, who came from across the sea to die in stinking loathsome squalor," said a seaman whose ship docked at the island. "What sorrows have been suffered here, what agonies endured, what deaths died!"

Was Dreyfus guilty or innocent? Someone had passed France's military secrets to the Germans; that much was known. But was it he?

Alfred Dreyfus, a captain in the French army and a Jew, was convicted of treason in 1895 and sentenced to life in prison on Devil's Island. The question of his guilt or innocence divided French society.

The question divided French society and came between relatives and friends. The fact that a court-martial had found Dreyfus guilty satisfied most people. Others—a minority known as *Dreyfusards*—believed in the captain's innocence. They pointed out that the army lacked good evidence against Dreyfus. He was being scapegoated, they argued, because of his faith. An American commentator summed up the situation this way: "In France to-day it is perilous to be a Jew."

Sarah Bernhardt proudly called herself a Dreyfusard. She stood firmly with Georges Clairin and her other friends who supported Dreyfus's cause. Yet the person who meant most to her, Maurice, believed Dreyfus was guilty. Sarah was outraged and argued with her son. Speaking up for Dreyfus was an act of patriotism, she said. No, to the contrary, questioning the army's verdict was unpatriotic, Maurice countered. Sarah insisted that Maurice be loyal to his own Jewish heritage. As for herself, "I am a daughter of the great Jewish race," she proclaimed. She had never practiced Judaism and still called herself a Catholic, but she felt linked by blood to the Jewish people. She had herself been the target of anti-Semitic slurs. It seemed to her that Maurice cared more about pleasing his high-society friends, who were all anti-Dreyfusards, than doing what was right. The fights drove mother and son apart. "I no longer know you," Sarah shouted at one Sunday dinner, throwing down her napkin. Maurice gathered his family and left. He moved with Terka and Simone to the south of France, far from his mother, and did not speak to her for more than a year.

Many French citizens wanted to forget Alfred Dreyfus and move on; the army certainly did. In 1896, when a letter was uncovered that identified the real spy, military leaders tried to suppress it. Bringing the truth to light would mean admitting that they had convicted the wrong man. But the Dreyfusards insisted that Dreyfus be remembered. On January 13, 1898, a Paris newspaper printed an open letter to the president of France. It was written by Émile Zola, a famous novelist.

The letter filled the paper's front page and caught the attention of the world. It was titled "*J'Accuse . . . !*"

Zola leveled one accusation after another, as if they were bullets fired from a gun. He accused the army and the government of repressing proof of Dreyfus's innocence. He accused them of conducting a deceitful inquiry and using the press to sway public opinion. He wrote, "I have but one passion, that of light, in the name of humanity, which has suffered so much and has a right to happiness. My fiery protest is nothing more than the cry of my soul."

Zola's letter brought an angry throng to the street outside his home. It was said that when a face appeared at his upstairs window, it belonged not to Zola but to Sarah Bernhardt. The sight of the great stage star calmed the crowd, which then dispersed. Whether or not this is true, Bernhardt did send a letter to Zola, thanking him "in the name of eternal justice." She wrote, "I am anguished, haunted by the situation." His beautiful words had given her hope.

Dreyfus proclaims his innocence in this pro-Dreyfusard artwork.

The publication of "*J'Accuse . . . !*" began a lengthy chain of events that led to Alfred Dreyfus being declared innocent, brought back from Devil's Island, and reinstated in the army eleven years after he was publicly degraded. Sarah and Maurice Bernhardt had patched up their relationship long before that day. Still, for years when they were together, they avoided mentioning the Dreyfus affair, knowing it could still draw heated words.

Why fight, anyway, when there were reasons to celebrate? In 1896, Terka and Maurice had a second daughter, named Lysiane. Then, later that year, the writers and artists of Paris organized an afternoon of festivities to honor Sarah Bernhardt.

On "Sarah Bernhardt Day," December 9, five hundred people in formal dress sat down together for a banquet luncheon at the Grand Hotel. Flowers, silver, and crystal covered the long tables. A spiral staircase descended into the great hall from an upper story, and all eyes watched as the guest of honor floated down. She was the "Queen of attitude and Princess of gestures," said the writer Edmond Rostand. At each curve in the staircase, Bernhardt halted briefly to strike a pose, bending over the railing or wrapping an arm around the central pillar. She was dressed like a queen, in a white dress with a long train, embroidered in gold and trimmed with lace and chinchilla. "Her lithe and slender body scarcely seemed to touch the earth. She was wafted towards us as it were in a halo of glory," wrote Jules Huret, a journalist. Bernhardt let no one see that her knee pained her at every step. During dessert, playwright Victorien Sardou offered a toast to "the great and the good Sarah." He spoke of having been fortunate "to see her in her home, among her children and her friends . . . to know the benevolence, the charity, and the exquisite kindness of the woman." With outstretched arms, Bernhardt thanked the crowd. "My heart, my whole heart is yours!" she gushed.

Following applause, tear-streaked cheeks, and a song sung by a choir, everyone moved to the Théâtre de la Renaissance. Hundreds of

Bernhardt descends a spiral staircase to join admirers who have gathered
to celebrate Sarah Bernhardt Day, December 9, 1896.

fans joined the luncheon guests to see the legendary Sarah Bernhardt perform scenes from *Phèdre* and *Rome vaincue*. Saradoteurs—students from the Conservatoire and local colleges—filled the balcony. "The whole audience was thrilled by her cries of anguish, the gestures of her hesitating arms, and the signs of grief upon her face," recalled Jules Huret. "I saw all my neighbours shed tears." The curtain rose again to reveal Bernhardt amid flowers, seated on a throne, and draped in a Grecian robe of white and gold. Around her were women in white with blossoms in their hair. One by one, seven poets came forward to recite sonnets they had written in Bernhardt's honor. "At this moment Sarah's emotion reached its height. She stood, with heaving breast, pale as the camellias about her," noted Huret. "No spectacle could be finer than this woman, whose unconquerable energy had withstood the struggles and difficulties of a thirty-years career, standing over-whelmed and vanquished by the power of a few lines of poetry."

Sarah Bernhardt would never forget this day. Knowing she had touched so many lives brought her deep happiness. She had worked hard throughout her career and had always been ambitious, and at fifty-two she continued to explore new roles. In *L'Aiglon,* by Edmond Rostand, she played a young man, Napoleon II, the only son of the emperor Napoleon. Nicknamed the Eaglet, Napoleon II lost his right of succession to the throne after his father's 1815 abdication.

What did she think about playing a male role? "A good actress, with the appearance befitting the part and the intelligence to comprehend it, can play the man as well as the woman. It is simply another char-acter for her to identify with herself," Bernhardt explained. A woman playing *L'Aiglon* "must actually *be* the boy, for the moment, not only to the spectators and her companions, but to herself as well," she contin-ued. "She must impress the onlookers not with the idea, 'How well she is taking a boy's part!' but, 'This *is L'Aiglon!*'"

Bernhardt immersed herself in the life and character of Napoleon

II. She described the hard work that went on behind the scenes as she brought this—or any—character to life: "When I undertake a new rôle I am that character for the time being. I study the physiology of the character and weld it out," she wrote. "I think and try to feel as the character would do under given circumstances. If it is a historical play, I read everything I can find concerning the period, the manners, customs, trend of thought, and mode of dress." There was hardly a moment when she was not preparing. "I will study in my carriage, in bed, when eating—all the time," she revealed. "Then, when the character is mine, it is ready at any time to be assumed like a costume, and it should be equally well-fitting."

Bernhardt in costume for one of her celebrated male roles, Napoleon II, L'Aiglon.

In May 1899, Bernhardt donned a cape, buckled on a sword, and appeared onstage as another male figure, Prince Hamlet, in a French translation of Shakespeare's great tragedy. Her fans in France were fascinated. Her old lover Jean Mounet-Sully, who had often played Hamlet at the Comédie-Française, came to see her perform the role ten times. Bernhardt took the production to England, where audiences were less kind. One British critic, known for his biting wit, titled his review "Hamlet, Princess of Denmark." He could never forget that the actor he saw on the stage was a woman. Other Britons thought that only an English actor could understand Shakespeare. Bernhardt disagreed, insisting that great art is for the whole world. "Shakespeare, by his colossal genius, belongs to the universe," she declared.

Hamlet was one of the first plays Bernhardt presented at a new theater, one she had leased and renovated. The Théâtre de la Renaissance, which held nine hundred seats, had been large. The new site, which she named the Théâtre Sarah Bernhardt, seated seventeen hundred people. Bernhardt could welcome more of her fans there, and she could earn more money. She had promised the public that the theater bearing her name would be beautiful, and it was. Yellow velvet covered its walls and seats, its balconies had been painted ivory, and glittering chandeliers hung from its high ceiling. The stage was spacious, and the star's two-story "dressing room" was more like a townhouse, with a luxurious sitting room, a kitchen, and a dining room that seated twelve.

Bernhardt had complete artistic control at her theater. She chose the plays to be performed, hired the actors, and served as director. She selected the costumes and sets. Productions at the Théâtre Sarah Bernhardt became known for their crowd scenes, in which many actors filled the stage, and their extravagant scenery, which some people called elegant and others insisted was overdone.

Sarah Bernhardt also pioneered a new form of entertainment, the motion picture. She first appeared onscreen in 1900, as Prince Hamlet

Sarah Bernhardt caused some controversy when she tackled
the role of Shakespeare's Hamlet.

fighting his final duel. In this nearly two-minute film, Bernhardt and
another actor, both in tights and capes, drew swords and fought as if
to the death. Unlike films made later, this one featured no close-ups or
scenes shot from differing angles. The camera stood in one spot and
captured the actors moving wordlessly onstage. Like all early films, it

was silent. At the film's close, as Hamlet is fatally stabbed, Bernhardt staggers, swoons, and collapses into the arms of waiting guards. They lower the prince's lifeless body to the floor and then carry it away.

Twelve years later, Bernhardt starred in a condensed motion-picture version of *La Dame aux camélias,* or *Camille,* capturing on film a role she had performed onstage more than three thousand times. Bernhardt made another film based on the life of Queen Elizabeth I of Great Britain. *Queen Elizabeth* was a hit with audiences not only in France but in Britain and America as well. "I have conquered a new world," Bernhardt said. "I rely for my immortality upon these records." She would make eleven movies in all.

Film brought Sarah Bernhardt to more people than could ever see her live onstage. "It must have seemed glorious to defy the limitations of space and have the whole world as her audience," commented one writer about Bernhardt. "Her art loses nothing in its transmission to the little strips of celluloid."

In 1905 and 1906, Bernhardt again toured the New World, beginning in South America. On her last night in Rio de Janeiro, she performed in *La Tosca.* When the moment came for Floria Tosca to jump to her death, Bernhardt noticed too late that the mattresses intended to cushion her fall were missing. Down she went onto a wooden floor, landing hard on her damaged right knee. Blinding pain shot through her body. Soon, her leg swelled alarmingly, and walking became impossible. Bernhardt rested on the twenty-day voyage to New York, but she had to spend several days in a hospital before she could use the leg again.

She still drew huge crowds in the United States. New Yorkers once more lined up for blocks to buy tickets for her shows. In Texas, a cowboy rode three hundred miles on horseback just to see the famous star. In Kansas City and Dallas, she appeared in a custom-made circus tent that held five thousand seats. Bernhardt was in the Midwest on April 18, 1906, when an earthquake and fire devastated San Francisco. She

Bernhardt portrayed Britain's Queen Elizabeth I in an early film.

learned with dismay that as many as three thousand people had died, and others had seen their homes destroyed. San Franciscans desperately needed food, clothing, and other supplies. To raise money for the victims, Bernhardt had her circus tent set up in Chicago and gave a benefit performance. Two weeks later, she was in the ravaged city, where she surveyed the damage from an open car. Because the people also needed the comfort that the arts provide, she gave a free performance of *Phèdre* at the Greek Theatre, an open-air amphitheater in nearby Berkeley, California.

The tour brought Bernhardt back to Montreal, where she was as controversial as ever. Even before she arrived, the Roman Catholic archbishop urged the faithful to stay home from her plays. Not only was Bernhardt a sinful woman, he warned, but staged plays in general

posed a "danger to morality." For young people, they offered "schooling in sin." Bernhardt would be presenting a new play that was especially evil, the archbishop said. *La Sorcière,* by Victorien Sardou, was
set in Spain in the sixteenth century, when the church executed people accused of heresy. That was a shameful chapter in church history,
and unsuitable entertainment for Catholics, the archbishop thought.
Again, Sarah Bernhardt turned out to be too strong a temptation. A
local newspaper reported that *La Sorcière* drew "the greatest audience
which ever saw a theatrical presentation in Montreal."

With the tour complete, Bernhardt came home to up-to-date, ever-
changing Paris. Since 1889, the city had a new landmark, the Eiffel
Tower, a wrought-iron spire rising more than a thousand feet into the
air. Paris-based artists such as Pablo Picasso and Henri Matisse were
experimenting with shapes and colors. "When I use a green it doesn't
mean grass. When I use a blue it doesn't mean the sky," Matisse wrote,
forcing the public to look at paintings in novel ways. Electric lights
were brightening rooms at night, and automobiles were rolling along
Paris boulevards, vying for space with horse-drawn carriages.

Time brought progress—as well as sorrow. In 1900, Madame
Guérard, Sarah's little lady, had died. She was such a private person that
her first name has long been forgotten. Even her death certificate iden-

People flock to Bernhardt's circus tent in Chicago. A photograph of Bernhardt as Hamlet has been superimposed on this panoramic picture.

tifies her simply as the "widow Guérard." Jeanne Bernhardt also died in that year, a victim of her drug habit. And in 1905, Jeanne's daughter, Saryta, succumbed to a lung condition. Companion, sister, niece: Sarah felt each of these deaths keenly. Life had taught her, though, that loss is a part of every relationship. She would carry on, *quand même*.

Then, in June 1910, Terka Bernhardt died of an unknown illness, leaving Maurice and their two daughters. Simone was already twenty-one and newly married, but Lysiane was still a teenager. In April 1911, missing a mother to confide in and ask for advice, Lysiane went to live with her welcoming grandmother. "I basked in the sunlight of her presence," wrote Lysiane. *Grand-mère* Sarah instructed Lysiane, "Do something with your ten fingers," preferring to see young people busy rather than idle. "So I took lessons in the piano, in drawing and in elocution," Lysiane recalled. Soon she had decorated the staircase at Bernhardt's home with portraits of dogs.

On March 6, 1914, it was the ringing doorbell that kept Lysiane busy. All day long, she accepted deliveries of flowers, telegrams, and letters of congratulations on behalf of her grandmother. They came from friends and colleagues as well as people who had never met the famous star. Sarah Bernhardt had been awarded France's highest commendation, the cross of a chevalier of the Legion of Honor, recognizing her

Friends and loved ones wish Bernhardt well as she receives the Legion of Honor,
France's highest decoration. To her right stands Maurice Bernhardt, a handsome
gentleman with graying hair. Her granddaughter Lysiane Bernhardt stands to
her left and somewhat behind her.

service to her country. For years she had brought pleasure to the people
of France through her acting. She had introduced audiences throughout the world to the works of renowned French dramatists. One journalist dubbed her "the greatest missionary whom France or any other
country has sent abroad." Another called her a living legend. "When
a person becomes legendary in life," he wrote, "legendary that person
remains unto the end."

NINE

A Flaming Heart

How wonderful she looked in those days!
She was as transparent as an azalea,
only more so; like a cloud, only not so thick.
Smoke from a burning paper describes
her more nearly . . . Her body was not
the prison of her soul, but its shadow.
—Ellen Terry, actor

A legend can also be a target. In September 1914, Bernhardt was at home with her family when an official from the Ministry of War paid a call. The government was advising Madame Sarah Bernhardt to leave the city, he said. The army had captured from the Germans a list of prominent people to be taken hostage if they invaded Paris, and her name was on it. For the second time in Bernhardt's life, France was at war.

The countries of Europe had been wary of one another since the end of the Franco-Prussian War, in 1871. They had chosen sides, hoping for strength in numbers in case fighting broke out again. With Great Britain and Russia, France formed the Triple Entente. The three nations promised to aid one another if attacked by some other power. A similar agreement, the Triple Alliance, made partners of Germany, Italy, and Austria-Hungary.

The Austro-Hungarian Empire encompassed Austria, Hungary, and several countries on the Balkan Peninsula. The empire's diverse population spoke a variety of languages and practiced different religions. Some of these people felt allegiance to lands beyond the empire's reaches and resented Austro-Hungarian rule. This was especially true of ethnic Serbs living in Bosnia, a Balkan region that Austria-Hungary annexed in 1908. They dreamed of seeing Bosnia freed from Austro-Hungarian control and united with Serbia, one Balkan country that remained independent.

Germany and Austria clasp hands in this sketch, signaling their close alliance.

La triple détente.

This political cartoon depicts a French wish, that the nations of the Triple Entente easily defeat Germany.

On June 28, 1914, a Bosnian Serb assassinated Archduke Franz Ferdinand, the heir to the Austrian throne. This one act was all it took to destroy peace in Europe. Austria-Hungary declared war on Serbia, thus angering Russia, which stood ready to protect the Serbs. The Russians had long desired dominance in the Balkan region and positioned their troops for a fight. Next, Germany declared war on Russia, a French ally, and then on France itself. The conflict would eventually grow to involve more nations, including the United States, and to be called the Great War, much later known as the First World War.

Once warned that she was in danger, Sarah Bernhardt wasted no time. She and her family left Paris by train for Andernos-les-Bains, a small bayside town in southwestern France. It was a quiet, out-of-the-way place where even someone as famous as Sarah Bernhardt might escape notice.

The trip was hard for Bernhardt to make. Not only did she have chronic pain in her right knee, but her doctor had encased her leg in a plaster cast. Dr. Samuel-Jean Pozzi hoped that keeping the leg immobile for six months might ease her constant discomfort. Pozzi had been Bernhardt's physician for many years. Long ago they had been lovers, and she counted him as a friend. She thought so highly of his medical knowledge that she called him Doctor God and followed his instructions to the letter. Pozzi suspected that Bernhardt had developed a form of arthritis in her damaged knee, although he could not be sure. Whatever was wrong with her leg, by January 1915, when the six months were up and the cast was removed, it was as painful as ever.

One morning in February, she asked Lysiane, Maurice, and his new wife, Marcelle, to come into her bedroom in the house where they were all staying. She had them sit down and announced that she had reached a decision. It was time for her leg to come off. "My mind is made up: I am not going on suffering," she said. Horrified, the others begged her to reconsider. Amputation was out of the question, Maurice said, and Dr. Pozzi agreed when Bernhardt expressed her wish in a letter. Surgery carried a risk of infection, and recovery was painful. It was a strain on any patient, but especially on one seventy years old. Nevertheless, Bernhardt persisted. "I have perhaps ten or fifteen years to live," she wrote to Pozzi. "Why condemn me to suffering another fifteen years? With a wooden leg I will be able to recite, maybe even perform." She added, "I don't want to lose my gaiety."

Pozzi referred the case to Dr. Jean-Paul Denucé, a respected surgeon practicing in Bordeaux, the nearest large city to Andernos-les-Bains. Denucé studied x-rays of Bernhardt's knee and agreed to do the procedure. So, on February 22, Bernhardt displayed bravery for her family, humming "La Marseillaise" as she was wheeled into the operating room. "Cheer up!" she called out. "In any case it is not so hard to have an amputation at my age as at the age of our children out there." The children she spoke of were the French soldiers who had lost arms or legs while fighting for their country.

The surgery took fifteen minutes. The patient recovered quickly and with no complications, but what happened to her amputated leg remains a mystery. Some people have claimed that the American showman P. T. Barnum offered ten thousand dollars for it; others have said that the planners of the 1915 Pan Pacific International Exposition in San Francisco asked to have it. In 2009, the hospital in Bordeaux announced that workers had found the leg in a storeroom. It turned

Sarah Bernhardt's surgery was front-page news throughout the world.

out, though, that the staff had come across an old left leg preserved in a jar, one that had been amputated below the knee. It was not Sarah Bernhardt's right leg, which had been cut off just above the knee.

In the months that followed, Bernhardt tried out several prosthetic legs, but she hated them all. In 1915, most artificial legs were carved from wood and were uncomfortable and stiff. World War I led to big improvements in prostheses to aid the many men who lost limbs in battle. These were often made from metal and jointed for more natural movement, but Bernhardt did without one. She preferred to be carried in a wooden sedan chair rather than walk from place to place. Free from pain at last, she was eager to be active, and to act again. "There is always a way," Bernhardt said. "In case of necessity I shall have myself strapped to the scenery."

She also wanted to help France win the war. French soldiers and their allies were facing the Germans along the Western Front, a line of muddy trenches fortified by barbed wire and machine guns. It stretched more than three hundred and fifty miles, from the Belgian coast to the Swiss border. France's losses were heavy, with little ground being gained, yet the Germans were failing to make real progress. The war felt like a stalemate, and people were discouraged.

With capture no longer a big risk, Bernhardt went home to Paris. On November 6, 1915, she returned to the stage in a new play created for her by the writer Eugène Morand. In *Les Cathédrales,* a soldier sleeps and dreams of France's monumental churches. Actors speak for the cathedrals and explain that, from one end of France to the other, they guard the nation's hope. Notre-Dame de Paris and the cathedrals of Bourges, Arles, Saint-Pol-de-Léon, and Amiens all have inspiring words to say.

Bernhardt gave her voice to Strasbourg Cathedral, which had been damaged by enemy guns in the Franco-Prussian War. The stage was arranged for her to say her lines while sitting down, since moving was so hard for her. Yet when she neared the end of her speech, she pulled herself up to her full height. "Weep, weep, Germany," her voice rang out. "The eagle, the German eagle has fallen into the Rhine!" The audience went wild. If Sarah Bernhardt could foresee Germany's defeat, then so could they. People left the theater with new optimism.

Les Cathédrales boosted public spirit, but Bernhardt hoped to do more for her country. When she learned that young actors from the Comédie-Française were planning to visit the war zone and perform for the fighting men, she offered to go along. The others

Les Cathédrales was staged to let Bernhardt play her role while seated.

hesitated; for entertainers to travel to the scene of war was something new, and it was likely to be dangerous. Bernhardt was ancient in their eyes, and she had a disability. Could she withstand the rigors of the Western Front? The young actors asked one another, "Why doesn't she retire?"

One of them, Béatrix Dussane, paid a call on Bernhardt to discuss the tour and spell out its hardships. A servant led her to a white bedroom, where the legendary star sat engulfed in a huge armchair. Dussane understood at once that she was face-to-face with an "extraordinary being." Her eyes took in "a thousand folds of satin and lace, a ruffle of red hair, ageless features, with all the wrinkles covered in makeup," she later wrote. Beholding the great woman who was now so small and weak, Dussane felt that she was looking at "a little pile of ashes." But what a pile of ashes! "For two hours she rehearsed, repeated her lines, practiced her movements, made cuts, ordered tea, asked about travel arrangements, was energetic, touched, amused. She saw all, heard all, understood all. For two hours, the little pile of ashes never stopped throwing off sparks." Dussane concluded that Bernhardt had the stamina to handle the trip: "I knew that she had been born this way, and she would be this way forever."

The troupe performed first in northeastern France, close to the fighting. Three thousand men were brought together in a covered market to see the show. Many wore bandages, evidence that they had been wounded in battle. As a makeshift curtain opened to reveal Sarah Bernhardt seated on a worn-out chair, they barely applauded. "Illustrious names meant nothing to them," Dussane knew. "Strong, reliable guys nurtured by the soil of France, they waited to see the show and make up their own minds." Bernhardt understood that she would have to win her audience over, and she did, as soon as she began speaking lines from *Les Cathédrales*. "Her speech was vibrant, rising like the sound of a battle charge. It recalled heroic figures planting a flag on conquered ground," Dussane observed. "To arms!" Bernhardt cried, and a band struck up "La Marseillaise." Three thousand soldiers rose to their feet to clap and cheer.

The performances continued. In hospital wards and army mess tents, in a packed barn, and on the terrace of an abandoned chateau, Béatrix Dussane had many chances to witness Bernhardt's bravery. It took courage not only to put herself within range of gunfire but also to keep up with a schedule and working conditions that were stressful for younger, stronger actors. "We who are near the end of life forget to fear," Bernhardt liked to say.

"Of all the images of Sarah," Dussane concluded, "the one that seems to me the greatest is that old woman of genius hobbling along in her little chair and on her poor leg, to give her flaming heart and her valiant smile to those who were suffering for us."

French soldiers wait in earthen trenches for the enemy's approach.

Bernhardt made a second trip to the front a few weeks later, with Lysiane coming along to help her. She acted for soldiers in the Marne region, east of Paris, where France and its allies had won a key battle and were holding the Germans back. She wanted to go into the trenches and meet the men where they lived and fought, but the army refused to let her.

She also starred in a motion picture. *Mères françaises* was a true-to-life drama that showed the crushing effects of war on one French village. Bernhardt played a woman who lost her husband and son in battle. Some of *Mères françaises* was filmed so close to the front lines that the actors could hear bursts of artillery fire.

Still Sarah Bernhardt needed to do more. She thought about a nation on the far side of the Atlantic Ocean, one that had resources and manpower to assist France, if only it would. The United States had thus far remained neutral, even though German submarines were targeting American commercial ships. In the fall of 1916, Bernhardt risked becoming a target of enemy torpedoes herself as she set sail for her final American tour. It would keep her away from France for two years. She was determined to change American minds, to make people understand the need to go to war. She traveled with several actors from her company and two dogs. Upon her arrival, a circus manager gave her a lion cub called Hernani, named for a play by Victor Hugo in which Bernhardt had starred.

Bernhardt acted scenes that allowed her to be seated, rather than entire plays. In the death scene from *Cleopatra,* for example, she reclined on a couch. Her days of acting in a circus tent belonged to the past. Now, in American cities and towns, Bernhardt often appeared in vaudeville theaters, sandwiched between comedians and acrobats. Before leaving the stage, she urged her American audiences to join the war effort. By the time she was through, patriotic cries rose from the stage and the seats: "Long live France; America for ever!" How many Americans Bernhardt persuaded cannot be known. She was still in

This poster advertises a performance at the Théâtre
Sarah Bernhardt to benefit men wounded in the war.

the United States on April 6, 1917, when the U.S. Congress declared
war on Germany.

Bernhardt had laid out a daunting schedule, planning to visit
ninety-nine cities and towns. For six months she was on the go, stopping in one city after another. Then, after performing in Saratoga
Springs, New York, she fell ill. A doctor at New York City's Mount
Sinai Hospital diagnosed an acute kidney infection. Again, Sarah

Bernhardt's health made news. People in the United States, Europe, and other lands read in their newspapers that she would have surgery, and that she sent a kiss to all her fans. Two days later, they learned that the operation was a success, and that Bernhardt's "Marvelous Vitality Gives Hope of Her Recovery." Despite the good news, her family worried. Maurice, Marcelle, and Lysiane sailed for New York, to be at her bedside while she healed. When the time came for them to go home, she asked Lysiane to stay. "Death had brushed her so closely that she dreaded the idea of being 'without a Bernhardt,'" Lysiane wrote.

Lysiane traveled by train with her grandmother to Chicago, Grand Rapids, New Orleans, San Francisco, and places in between. They sailed to Havana, Cuba, and ventured from British Columbia to Ontario and Quebec, in Canada. In Los Angeles, Sarah and Lysiane rode in a parade held to encourage people to buy war bonds.

Bernhardt's animals had caused trouble in the past, and Hernani, the lion cub, was no exception. He grew bigger every day and reminded his human companions that he was a wild beast at heart. Not only did he eat raw meat, but he tore up curtains and relieved himself on carpets. Pretty soon no hotel would welcome him. A reluctant Bernhardt had no choice but to send him back to the circus and hope he would be happier there.

Sarah and Lysiane Bernhardt had booked passage home on a ship sailing from New York, the *Espagne*. As they were about to board, an American soldier came forward and introduced himself. His name, he said, was Robert Markero. The women looked puzzled, so he said that he had been born on the *Amérique* in 1880. Of course! He was the baby Bernhardt had helped bring into the world on her first voyage to America, all grown up. Sarah Bernhardt hugged her godson, who told her that he was headed to his home in Nevada. He, too, had lost a leg, while battling in France.

In Boston during her final American tour, Bernhardt met the famed illusionist Harry Houdini and his wife. Houdini was renowned for his sensational escapes, for freeing himself from chains, handcuffs, and locked trunks, for example, or digging himself out of the earth after being buried alive. "You do such wonderful things. Could you bring back my leg for me?" Bernhardt asked. Houdini admitted to the star that the magic she asked for was beyond his power.

The ship's captain assigned two sailors to escort Bernhardt, to ensure that she traveled safely. But she insisted that she needed no special attention. "Do you imagine for one moment that I would allow those boys to bother about me if we were torpedoed?" she asked Lysiane. "At my age!"

No German submarines spotted the *Espagne,* which reached France safely on November 11. The passengers had heard no news in their nine days at sea, and they all wondered about the progress of the war.

Parisians take to the streets to celebrate the end of World War I.

Standing on the deck as the ship steamed into port, Lysiane listened as people on the pier shouted a single word: Armistice! The gangplank was lowered, and Lysiane spotted her father hurrying aboard. Maurice Bernhardt did not see her as he pushed his way through passengers lined up to go ashore. He made his way to the cabin where Sarah Bernhardt waited to be helped. "Mama!" he cried. "It's the armistice! The war is over!" Sarah cried tears of joy. She was in the arms of her beloved Maurice, and France and its allies had won.

TEN

WOUNDED BIRD

This is Sarah! And glory to her!

* * *

she shines in the world's eyes
with the brilliance of a star.
—Rubén Darío, poet

Sarah Bernhardt was in her seventies and as determined as ever to do things with her ten fingers. Running the Théâtre Sarah Bernhardt, a full-time job for anyone, was not enough. "I must try to be useful," she said. With a lifetime of knowledge to share, she held acting classes at the theater. Those who came to learn sat in a wide semicircle onstage, and Bernhardt perched behind a table. She hated chilly drafts, so she wrapped herself in a chinchilla coat and covered her lap with a robe. She sipped from a glass of milk and sniffed a perfumed handkerchief to revive her energy.

Never moving from her seat, she went over plays line by line, giving her class "the thought behind the words," as a student named May Agate phrased it. Mastering a role "had to be done through heart, mind, and understanding," Bernhardt said. Every emotion displayed onstage had to be authentic. "You must weep real tears, suffer real anguish, laugh a real laugh which is contagious," she taught. "We must make our characters live."

"What appealed to me in her teaching," said Agate, "was the extraordinary application of common sense to the interpretation of every line, so that it never ceased to be a human being speaking, however flowery the language might be." There was no room for laziness in Bernhardt's classes. "You had to think, and think hard, all the time," noted Agate, who went on to have a successful career in England. Bernhardt saved her strongest criticism for the students with the most potential. She pushed them to reach deep into themselves and bring forth their best.

Bernhardt also wrote. She published a memoir, *My Double Life,* recalling her private and public selves, from childhood through her first American tour. She authored a romance novel, *The Idol of Paris.* She also collected her thoughts on the craft of acting and put them into another book, *The Art of the Theatre.*

Acting, her life's work, was harder to do. A few playwrights created dramas especially for her, works that let her act while sitting or lying down. In *Daniel,* by Louis Verneuil (who was soon to be Lysiane's husband), Bernhardt again played a man, a morphine addict at the end of his life. She presented *Daniel* on her last trip to London, in April 1921. The curtain opened to reveal her seated on a high-backed chair, wrapped in an invalid's dressing gown. Chalky makeup gave her a deathly pallor; her blackened eyes looked sunken.

Like many of the other characters Bernhardt portrayed in her long career, Daniel dies at the end of the play. "It was not an agonised death, but a quietly pathetic fading away during the reading of a letter," commented a writer who was present. It was a gentle death, and a convincing one. "Again the great actress had the audience, as the saying is, in the hollow of her hand." The curtain fell, and "the enthusiasm knew no bounds. The cheering went on and on," the writer continued. "Only

Seated in her sedan chair, Bernhardt is carried ashore at Dover in 1921,
at the start of her final trip to England.

an artist of indisputable genius could have roused an audience as
Mme. Sarah Bernhardt did."

Sarah Bernhardt was loved by many. Older fans recalled her when
she was in her prime; younger ones saw her as a living legend, a symbol of France. She could still fill theaters and earn loud applause, but
tastes were changing. Bernhardt's flamboyant of acting, which had

seemed fresh and natural when she was young, appeared dated and overly dramatic to new generations of theatergoers. Tragedies befalling queens in jeweled costumes had gone out of fashion. Melodramas like *La Dame aux camélias* belonged to an earlier century.

Most modern people preferred plays by writers such as Henrik Ibsen and Anton Chekhov, which probed the psychology of ordinary women and men and found drama in everyday life. They praised performers such as Eleonora Duse of Italy, who held audiences rapt with her tender gaze. Duse's fans insisted that in her plain costumes and simple makeup, she was just as majestic as Bernhardt.

Sacha Guitry, a young writer who had known Bernhardt since he was a child, wrote a play titled *Un Sujet de roman* with a part especially for her. Guitry's father was also cast in this drama, playing Bernhardt's character's husband. Lucien Guitry had shared the stage with Bernhardt many times over the years, and he had also shared her bed. He knew her well and remained fond of her. In December 1922, during a rehearsal, the two practiced an emotional scene in which the estranged husband and wife reach a new understanding. "Sarah was at the peak of her powers that day," Sacha Guitry remembered, although she looked frail and suddenly old. The people close to Bernhardt knew that she was unwell. In truth, her kidneys were failing. There was no treatment for this dangerous condition in 1922, which meant that her health could only deteriorate.

"She spoke in a terrifyingly thin, disjointed, magnificent, heart-rending voice," Sacha Guitry noted. Lucien Guitry sat across from her at a table with a hat pulled over his eyes. It was his turn to speak, but instead he took Bernhardt's hand. "He could not go on. He was weep-ing," Sacha Guitry knew. When the rehearsal ended, Bernhardt asked to rest in a dressing room. In a little while she began to cough and choke and had to be taken home. She never returned to the theater. Her years of acting onstage were behind her. Someone else would star

An aged Bernhardt was photographed near the end of her life with
a bust of Edmond Rostand that she created.

in Sacha Guitry's play, and trusted colleagues would manage the Théâtre Sarah Bernhardt.

Maurice and Lysiane begged Bernhardt to retire, but she would hear nothing of it. In early 1923, she started work on a moving picture, *La Voyante*. She was too ill to go out, so the film crew built a studio in her home, complete with the bright lights needed for filming and a painted backdrop showing a view of Paris. Bernhardt rested in her bedroom until it was time to play a scene and then was carried downstairs to face the camera. When she felt too sick to be moved, the crew went upstairs and filmed her in bed. But her condition worsened until any acting at all became too much of a strain, and another performer took over the role.

For two months, Bernhardt hung on to life. Maurice and other loved ones took care of her as she lay on pillows embroidered with the words *Quand Même*. A physician, Dr. Marot, came regularly. (Dr. Pozzi had died in 1918.) Her breathing grew labored, and on the afternoon of March 25, a Roman Catholic priest was summoned to administer last rites. As word spread that Sarah Bernhardt was slipping away, people gathered to hold a vigil in the boulevard Pereire. "I'll keep them dangling," Bernhardt joked as Maurice held her in his arms. She never spoke again.

On March 26, late in the day, Lysiane and her sister, Simone, stood at their grandmother's bedside. Maurice, who was exhausted, dozed in a chair. Lysiane placed a hand over Bernhardt's heart. "Through the white silk of her nightgown I felt it flutter softly, so softly, like a wounded bird trying to fly away," Lysiane wrote. "And then nothing. Nothing more." At 8 p.m., Dr. Marot opened a bedroom window and told the people below, "Madame Sarah Bernhardt is dead." The great Sarah Bernhardt was seventy-eight.

At just that moment, the curtain was going up at her theater.

The play being staged was *L'Aiglon*, in which Bernhardt had famously portrayed Napoleon II. Act 1 was under way when news of her death came. The performance stopped; the curtain fell; and the audience filed out, barely making a sound. The actors, still in their costumes and makeup, left immediately for Bernhardt's home to say their goodbyes.

For three days, life in Paris halted. So many people had seen Bernhardt onstage or onscreen, or had read about her adventures, that Parisians felt they had known her. How strange it was to think that she was dead!

Thousands of mourners filed past Bernhardt's deathbed. They saw her laid out in a white robe with the medal of the Legion of Honor on her chest. She had asked to be surrounded by flowers, and she was. Lilacs, roses, orchids, and carnations were everywhere. Thousands more admirers lined avenues on the day of her funeral, to kneel and weep as the horse-drawn hearse passed by. She was to be laid to rest

People fill the streets of Paris to see Bernhardt's flower-laden funeral procession pass by.

in her own coffin, the one in which she was photographed so many years before. The funeral cortege brought the star's remains first to the Church of Saint François de Sales for a funeral Mass, and then to Père Lachaise Cemetery, where her family members and many notable people were buried. The procession stopped briefly in front of the theater that bore her name, as if giving her time to say *adieu*.

Edmond Rostand's son, Maurice Rostand, was moved to see the crowd following Bernhardt's cortege. "But I was infinitely more moved," he said, "when I saw her die, even for the hundredth time, on stage."

Near the end of her life, Sarah Bernhardt invited the writer Colette to lunch. Two generations younger than her host, Colette was known for books that explored love and women's lives. She had seen Bernhardt onstage, but never up close. At lunch she studied the star's small hands, which made Colette think of faded blossoms. "I could have gazed forever into the blue of her eyes as they changed their tint in accordance with all the movements, still so full of life, of that tiny and imperious head," Colette recalled.

The women talked about the theater. When they had finished eating, Bernhardt served coffee to her guest. Colette never would forget "the delicate and withered hand offering the brimming cup, the flowery azure of the eyes, so young still in their network of fine lines." Bernhardt's body had aged, but her spirit remained youthful. She was as determined as ever to win the love of an audience, even an audience of one. Colette saw this in her eyes, in the playful, flirty tilt of her head, and in "that indestructible desire to charm, to charm still, to charm right up to the gates of death itself."

Sarah Bernhardt, 1844–1923.

AUTHOR'S NOTE

Speculation passes as fact in some accounts of Sarah Bernhardt's life. The confusion begins with her birthdate, which Bernhardt claimed was October 22, 1844. It cannot be verified, because her birth certificate was destroyed, but we can safely say that she was born on or near that date.

What about her name? Some books state with authority that her "real name" was Rosine Henriette Bernhardt. Their authors base this claim on her application to the Conservatoire, where this name appears. Yet her baptismal certificate identifies her differently, as Sarah Marie Henriette Bernhardt. Did her mother give her one of those names when she was born? Or did Youle Van Hard call her oldest daughter something else? Again, without the birth certificate as proof, it is impossible to know.

Some sources claim that Sarah's father was one Édouard Bernhardt, because the baptismal certificate identifies him in that way. These writers apparently overlooked the fact that Youle Van Hard had a brother with that name. Van Hard could have used her brother's name for the sake of convenience, to avoid identifying Sarah's real father, or for some other reason of her own. Our knowledge of the past is incomplete. At times historians and biographers must acknowledge that they don't have all the answers.

The myths about Bernhardt that circulated in and outside of France present another challenge. Sarah Bernhardt was so famous in her day, and lived so unconventionally, that many people were willing to believe anything they read about her, no matter how far-fetched it was. Bernhardt supposedly had more illustrious lovers than anyone could count; her alleged antics included charging people money to see her in men's clothing; not only did she take boxing lessons, but she punched the boxing teacher in the face and broke his teeth. Also, Bernhardt herself invented stories about her early life, and she embellished past events when describing them to listeners. The tall tales belong in an account of Sarah Bernhardt's life—if we recognize them for what they are. Not only did they add to the aura that surrounded her, but they are keys to her character. They are part of the fun in reading about such a grand, extraordinary person.

Sarah Bernhardt, in a photograph taken around 1880.

Sarah Bernhardt and Madame Guérard were devoted to each other for many years. The dog is one of many that Bernhardt befriended and cared for.

Notes

"The nineteenth century will be called": Mary Louise Roberts, *Disruptive Acts*, 221.

PROLOGUE
Face-to-Face

1   "There are five kinds of actresses": Arthur Gold and Robert Fizdale, *The Divine Sarah*, 3.

"She was not pretty": F. H. Duquesnel, "Les Débuts de Sarah Bernhardt," 1.

2   "I have touched real death": Sarah Bernhardt, *The Art of the Theatre*, 78.

5   "What I am trying to show you": "Miscellanea," 335.

ONE
What Can Be Done with Sarah?

7   "Meek, / Chic": "An Ode to Sara."

10   p. "Honest work would never have brought me": Joanna Richardson, *The Courtesans*, 154.

"black, black!": Sarah Bernhardt, *My Double Life*, 3.

12   "in a beautiful, wide bed": Ibid., 5.

13   "I would then rush about": Ibid., 10.

14   "And to think that this": Robert Gottlieb, *Sarah*, 13.

"Why had my mother been so cruel": Ibid.

15   "The idea that I was to be ordered about": Sarah Bernhardt, *My Double Life*, 11.

"the sweetest and merriest face": Ibid., 17.

16 "I became a personality": Ibid., 25.

19 "There it is": Ibid., 42.

22 "As we have come here": Ibid., 51.

"as though I was": Ibid., 45.

TWO
FRANCE'S GREATEST ACTOR-IN-TRAINING

23 "The art of acting": "To Sarah Bernhardt," *The Palace Theater Presents Madame Sarah Bernhardt in Vaudeville*, unnumbered page.

25 "Do you know": Sarah Bernhardt, *My Double Life*, 52.

"The Conservatoire!": Ibid.

"Why, she's as ugly as a louse": Ruth Brandon, *Being Divine*, 39.

"I had been discussed": Sarah Bernhardt, *My Double Life*, 56.

27 "If my rival I embrace": Jean Racine, *Britannicus*, 305.

"Tyrant, why leave thy butchery": Pierre Corneille, *Polyeucte*, 113.

28 "Is this a joke": Gottlieb, *Sarah*, 22.

"Two Doves, twin-brothers": Jean de La Fontaine, *Fables from La Fontaine*, 295.

"Are you a Jewess?": Gottlieb, *Sarah*, 22.

"By birth, sir": Ibid., 22–23.

"She's been baptized": Ibid., 23.

"I was mad": Gold and Fizdale, *The Divine Sarah*, 42.

"by the extension of one arm": Shearer West, *The Image of the Actor*, 106.

"throw the body": Sarah Bernhardt, *The Art of the Theatre*, 114.

"Oh, that one": Ibid., 115.

31 "little rebel": Sarah Bernhardt, *My Double Life*, 44.

32 "there's a role": Gottlieb, *Sarah*, 25.

"I fell on my knees": Sarah Bernhardt, *My Double Life*, 75.

34 "It was only just": Ibid.

"I looked perfectly hideous": Ibid., 81.

"Poor child": Ibid., 83.

35 "You were a failure": Ibid., 89.

"Had there been any poison": Mme. Pierre Berton, *The Real Sarah Bernhardt, Whom Her Audiences Never Knew*, 101.

"Do not worry any more": Sarah Bernhardt, *My Double Life*, 90.

THREE
STEPPING ONTO THE WORLD'S STAGE

36 "Those amazingly blue eyes": Berton, *The Real Sarah Bernhardt, Whom Her Audiences Never Knew*, 30.

"My mother isn't married": Gottlieb, *Sarah*, 30.

37 "She holds herself well": Ibid., 35.

"This performance was a very poor business": Ibid.

"I was insignificant": Brandon, *Being Divine*, 63.

"See! The whole world": Gottlieb, *Sarah*, 35.

39 "You miserable creature!": Sarah Bernhardt, *My Double Life*, 101.

"You'll spoil my make-up!": Ibid., 102.

"I did not do it": Ibid.

"I will leave": Ibid., 108.

40 "I thought too": Ibid.

41 "Here, read that": Ibid., 107.

"vile temper": Ibid., 108.

42 "My poor child": Ibid., 110.

"Have pity": Ibid., 112.

44 "I forgot Paris": Ibid.,115.

"My mother looked very white": Ibid., 116.

45 "Take me with you": Ibid., 118.

"Oh, take her": Ibid.

"I was perfectly stupefied": Ibid.

"I know a woman": Gottlieb, *Sarah*, 43.

47 "You've got to calm down": Ibid., 45.

"You know, it's Duquesnel": Ibid., 46.

"And if it had been you": Ibid.

48 "Oh those traditions": Sarah Bernhardt, *The Art of the Theatre*, 122.

49 "Do you think": Gold and Fizdale, *The Divine Sarah*, 71–72.

50 "What can be said": François Coppée, *Souvenirs d'un Parisien*, 95.

52 "I was absolutely ruined": Sarah Bernhardt, *My Double Life*, 144.

FOUR

Under Siege

53 "You are lauded": "To Sara B," 4.

54 "How differently things turn out": Sarah Bernhardt, *My Double Life*, 147.

"They do well": George Sand, *Agendas*, vol. 4, 244.

55 "Everyone's acting": Ibid., 248.

"Young and charming": Gottlieb, *Sarah*, 53.

56 "The capture of Paris": Douglas Fermer, *France at Bay*, 12.

58 "as far as ever": Alistair Horne, *The Fall of Paris*, 65.

"I decided to use my strength": Sarah Bernhardt, *My Double Life*, 160.

60 "eight days without *café au lait*": Horne, *The Fall of Paris*, 177.

"This morning I regaled myself": Ross King, *The Judgment of Paris*, 287.

"one continuous noise": Henry Du Pré Labouchère, *Diary of the Besieged Resident in Paris*, 317.

61 "took her role more than seriously": Brandon, *Being Divine*, 138.

"Ah, what a horrible memory!": Gottlieb, *Sarah*, 56.

62 "Holding out was no longer possible": King, *The Judgment of Paris*, 294.

"a terrible sadness": Joanna Richardson, *Sarah Bernhardt and Her World*, 45.

63 "I preferred dying": Sarah Bernhardt, *My Double Life*, 192.

"I found all my adored ones": Ibid., 215.

64 "the struggle of the future": Donny Gluckstein, *The Paris Commune*, 154.

"No man of good sense": Paul Martine, *Souvenirs d'un insurgé*, 222.

"There has been nothing": David McCullough, *The Greater Journey*, 324.

"What blood and ashes": Sarah Bernhardt, *My Double Life*, 224.

65 "I shook out my hair": Ibid.

66 "There was a moderation": Ibid., 228.

"Oh, those rehearsals": Ibid., 229.

"All her movements": F. Sarcey, Comédiens et comediennes, vol. 1, 14–15.

FIVE
A Strange Girl in the Belle Époque

69 "She speaks entirely too fast": Francisque Sarcey, *Quarante ans de théâtre*, 101.

71 "deep, shining, liquid eyes": Richardson, *Sarah Bernhardt and Her World*, 48.

72 "To simulate blindness": untitled commentary in the *Nation*, November 16, 1876, 301.

"I gave myself entirely": Gottlieb, *Sarah*, 68.

73 "There were the stout bankers": Sarah Bernhardt, *The Art of the Theatre*, 24.

74 "If we could love": Anne Penesco, *Mounet-Sully*, 103.

"Unlike the other actresses": Mme. Octave Feuillet, *Souvenirs et correspondances*, 317–18.

75 "She has in a supreme degree": Henry James, *The Portable Henry James*, 546.

76 "It's not a funeral": Gold and Fizdale, *The Divine Sarah*, 115.

"These come in and out": "Mdlle. Sarah Bernhardt," 329–30.

"Is it a drawing-room": Ibid., 330.

78 "She was discovered": Lysiane Bernhardt, *Sarah Bernhardt*, 162.

80 "Be careful": Gold and Fizdale, *The Divine Sarah*, 143.

81 "There goes your star": Ibid., 144.

"I find a sky": Sarah Bernhardt, *In the Clouds*, 6.

83 "Vive Sarah Bernhardt": Sarah Bernhardt, *My Double Life*, 297.

"You shall see": Ibid., 307.

"I suffered, I wept": Ibid.

85 "The intensity, the ecstasy": James, *The Portable Henry James*, 545.

"She seemed like a leaf": Brandon, *Being Divine*, 229.

"My poor Skeleton": Sarah Bernhardt, *My Double Life*, 327.

SIX

WORLD-FAMOUS

87 "I've seen Bernhardt": "To Mme. Bernhardt," clipping from an unidentified American newspaper of the early twentieth century.

"I strode to the footlights": Gold and Fizdale, *The Divine Sarah*, 156.

88 "Never has an audience been so moved": Gottlieb, *Sarah*, 79–80.

"I do not want to die!" Eugène Scribe and Ernest Legouvé, *Adrienne Lecouvreur*, 78.

"burst into sobs and ovations": Gottlieb, *Sarah*, 79.

90   "I drink to France": Gold and Fizdale, *The Divine Sarah*, 160.

"Yes, let us drink": Ibid.

"The ability to do as I wanted": Gottlieb, *Sarah*, 80.

92   "Very much hurt": Sarah Bernhardt, *My Double Life*, 354

"I went at once": Ibid., 355.

"Divine Sarah": Cornelia Otis Skinner, *Madame Sarah*, 209.

"as lightly and as rapidly": "Sarah Bernhardt," *Gouverneur Herald*, November 4, 1880, 2.

94   "I am dying": Alexandre Dumas, Jr., *La Dame aux camélias*, 135.

"had never possessed beauty": Marie Colombier, *Le Voyage de Sarah Bernhardt en Amérique*, 56–57.

"She would appear young": *Theatre Magazine*, March 15, 1890, 308.

96   "wonderful blue eyes": Sarah Bernhardt, *My Double Life*, 377.

"I made such an effort": Ibid., 378.

"The deafening sound": Ibid.

97   "Both English and French": Ramon Hathorn, "Sarah Bernhardt and the Bishops of Montreal and Quebec," 99.

98   "The most extensively advertised woman": Patricia Marks, *Sarah Bernhardt's First American Theatrical Tour*, 69.

99   "My conscience was by no means tranquil": Sarah Bernhardt, *My Double Life*, 416.

"Come back, Sarah": Gold and Fizdale, *The Divine Sarah*, 187.

101   "I made up my mind": Richardson, *Sarah Bernhardt and Her World*, 102.

SEVEN

PUBLIC WOMAN/PRIVATE LIFE

102   "Sarah Bernhardt has taken a master": Roberts, *Disruptive Acts*, 184.

"Damala was the most cold-blooded": Gottlieb, *Sarah*, 115.

"I am acquainted": "Notes from Paris," 512.

103 "He looked like a dead man": Bram Stoker, *Personal Reminiscences of Henry Irving*, 345–46.

"charming and fresh": Ibid., 346.

"Damala! There he is": Édouard Noël and Edmond Stoullig. *Les Annales du théâtre et de la musique*, vol. 8, 299.

"His inexperience is colossal": Ibid.

104 "The great Sarah": Sarcey, *Quarante ans de théâtre*, 101.

105 "France, which treats my wife": Brandon, *Being Divine*, 307.

"My husband had spurned": Lysiane Bernhardt, *Sarah Bernhardt*, 162.

106 "miserly Jewess": Marie Colombier, *Les Mémoires de Sarah Barnum*, 159.

"Madame . . . if you have a gentleman friend": *Affaire Marie Colombier–Sarah Bernhardt*, 8.

"If I have a quarrel": Ibid., 9.

"Sarah Bernhardt would have done better": Ibid., 54.

107 "And who created": Ibid., 61.

"She is the drama": Rubén Darío, "El Estreno de Sarah Bernhardt."

108 "the youngest grandmother": Brandon, *Being Divine*, 323.

109 "the widow Damala": Gold and Fizdale, *The Divine Sarah*, 240.

110 "strong personality": "Madame Sarah Bernhardt—At Home in Sydney," 127.

111 "superb, simply superb": Brandon, *Being Divine*, 317.

112 "It is not easy": Reynaldo Hahn, *La Grande Sarah*, 141.

115 "We give ourselves over": Ibid., 144.

"was irresistibly comic": Maurice Baring, *The Puppet Show of Memory*, 217–18.

EIGHT

The Great and Good Sarah

116   "You know well": Gold and Fizdale, *The Divine Sarah*, 264.

     "In the name of the people": "A Modern Tragedy," 640.

     "They are degrading": Martin P. Johnson, *The Dreyfus Affair*, 32.

117   "Here are Men in Hell": W. E. Allison-Booth, *Devil's Island*, 1.

118   "In France to-day": John T. Morse, Jr., "The Dreyfus and Zola Trials."

     "I am a daughter": Gottlieb, *Sarah*, 154.

     "I no longer know you": Ibid.

119   "I have but one passion": Émile Zola, "J'Accuse . . . !"

     "in the name of eternal justice": Gold and Fizdale, *The Divine Sarah*, 277–78.

120   "Queen of attitude": Ibid., 263.

     "Her lithe and slender body": Jules Huret, *Sarah Bernhardt*, 161.

     "the great and the good Sarah": Ibid., 162.

     "My heart, my whole heart": Ibid.

122   "The whole audience was thrilled": Ibid., 167.

     "At this moment": Ibid., 169–70.

     "A good actress": Sarah Bernhardt, "Men's Rôles as Played by Women," 2114.

123   "When I undertake": Ibid.

124   "Hamlet, Princess of Denmark": Gottlieb, *Sarah*, 144.

     "Shakespeare, by his colossal genius": Gold and Fizdale, *The Divine Sarah*, 282.

126   "I have conquered": David W. Menefee, *Sarah Bernhardt in the Theatre of Films and Sound Recordings*, 92.

"it must have seemed glorious": David W. Menefee, *The First Female Stars*, 35.

128 "danger to morality": Hathorn, "Sarah Bernhardt and the Bishops of Montreal and Quebec," 105.

"the greatest audience": Ibid., 106.

"When I use a green": "Paris 1905–15."

129 "I basked in the sunlight": Lysiane Bernhardt, *Sarah Bernhardt*, 195.

"Do something with your ten fingers": Ibid., 196.

"So I took lessons": Ibid.

130 "the greatest missionary": "The Legend of Sarah Bernhardt," 434.

"When a person becomes legendary": Ibid., 433.

NINE
A Flaming Heart

131 "How wonderful she looked": Ellen Terry, *The Story of My Life*, 237.

134 "My mind is made up": Lysiane Bernhardt, *Sarah Bernhardt*, 211.

"I have perhaps ten or fifteen years": Caroline de Costa and Francesca Miller, "Sarah Bernhardt's Missing Leg," 284.

"I don't want to lose": Gottlieb, *Sarah,* 167.

"Cheer up": Lysiane Bernhardt, *Sarah Bernhardt*, 212.

136 "There is always a way": Gottlieb, *Sarah*, 170.

137 "Weep, weep, Germany": Eugène Morand, *Les Cathédrales*, 44.

138 "Why doesn't she retire?": Béatrix Dussane, *Reines de théâtre*, 210.

"extraordinary being": Ibid., 211.

"Illustrious names": Ibid., 213.

"Her speech was vibrant": Ibid.

139 "To arms!": Morand, *Les Cathédrales*, 46.

139 "We who are near the end": Charles Henry Meltzer, "Sarah Bernhardt as Her Friends Have Known Her," 430.

"Of all the images": Dussane, *Reines de théâtre*, 215.

140 "Long live France; America": Lysiane Bernhardt, *Sarah Bernhardt*, 217.

142 "Marvelous Vitality": *New York Times*, April 20, 1917.

"Death had brushed her": Lysiane Bernhardt, *Sarah Bernhardt*, 217.

143 "You do such wonderful things": John Kobler, "Bernhardt in America."

"Do you imagine": Ibid., 221.

144 "Mama! It's the armistice": Ibid., 222.

TEN
WOUNDED BIRD

145 "This is Sarah": Rubén Darío, *Teatros*, 10.

"I must try to be useful": Sarah Bernhardt, *The Art of the Theatre*, 13.

"the thought behind the words": May Agate, *Madame Sarah*, 28.

"had to be done": Ibid.

146 "You must weep": Sarah Bernhardt, *The Art of the Theatre*, 200–01.

"What appealed to me": Agate, *Madame Sarah*, 45.

"It was not an agonised death": Archibald Haddon, *Green Room Gossip*, 256.

"Only an artist of indisputable genius": Ibid., 255.

148 "Sarah was at the peak of her powers": Gold and Fizdale, *The Divine Sarah*, 328.

"She spoke in a terrifyingly thin": Ibid.

150 "I'll keep them dangling": Gottlieb, *Sarah*, 208.

"Through the white silk": Lysiane Bernhardt, *Sarah Bernhardt*, 227.

"Madame Sarah Bernhardt is dead": Gottlieb, *Sarah*, 208.

152　"but I was infinitely more moved": Danièle Déon-Bessière, *Les Femmes et la Légion d'honneur*, 50.

"I could have gazed forever": Colette, *Earthly Paradise*, 290.

"the delicate and withered hand": Ibid., 291.

"that indestructible desire to charm": Ibid.

BIBLIOGRAPHY

Affaire Marie Colombier–Sarah Bernhardt: Pièces a conviction. Paris: En Vente Chez Tous les Libraires, 1884.

Agate, May. *Madame Sarah*. New York: Benjamin Blom, 1969.

Allison-Booth, W. E. *Devil's Island: Revelations of the French Penal Settlements in Guiana*. London: Putnam, 1931.

Baring, Maurice. *The Puppet Show of Memory*. Boston: Little, Brown and Co., 1922.

Bernhardt, Lysiane. *Sarah Bernhardt: My Grandmother*. London: Hurst and Blackett, 1949.

Bernhardt, Sarah. *The Art of the Theatre*. London: Geoffrey Bles, 1924.

———. *In the Clouds*. New York: Seaside Library, 1880.

———. "Men's Rôles as Played by Women." *Harper's Bazaar*, December 15, 1900, 2113–15.

———. *My Double Life: Memoirs of Sarah Bernhardt*. London: William Heinemann, 1907.

Berton, Mme. Pierre. *The Real Sarah Bernhardt, Whom Her Audiences Never Knew*. New York: Boni and Liveright, 1924.

Brandon, Ruth. *Being Divine: A Biography of Sarah Bernhardt*. London: Secker and Warburg, 1991.

Carlson, Marvin. *The French Stage in the Nineteenth Century*. Metuchen, NJ: Scarecrow Press, 1972.

Colette. *Earthly Paradise*. London: Secker and Warburg, 1966.

Colombier, Marie. *Les Mémoires de Sarah Barnum*. Paris: Chez Tous les Libraires, 1883.

———. *Le Voyage de Sarah Bernhardt en Amérique*. Paris: Maurice Dreyfous, 1881.

Coppée, François. *Souvenirs d'un Parisien*. Paris: Alphonse Lemerre, 1910.

Corneille, Pierre. *Polyeucte*. Auckland, New Zealand: The Floating Press, 2010.

de Costa, Caroline, and Francesca Miller. "Sarah Bernhardt's Missing Leg." *Lancet*, July 25, 2009, 284–85.

Darío, Rubén. "El Estreno de Sarah Bernhardt." *Cuentosinfin*. (www.cuentosinfin. com/el-estreno-de-sarah-bernhardt; accessed July 22, 2018)

———. *Teatros: La Tournée de Sarah Bernhardt en Chile.* Managua: Ricardo Llopesa, 2000.

Déon-Bessière, Danièle. *Les Femmes et la Légion d'honneur.* Paris: Les Éditions de l'Officine, 2002.

Dumas, Alexandre, Jr. *La Dame aux camélias.* Cincinnati: T. Wrightson and Co., 1856.

Duquesnel, F. H. "Les Débuts de Sarah Bernhardt." *Le Figaro*, September 16, 1894, 1.

Dussane, Béatrix. *Reines de théâtre.* Lyon, France: Protat Frères, 1944.

Fenby, Jonathan. *France: A Modern History from the Revolution to the War with Terror.* New York: St. Martin's Press, 2015.

Fermer, Douglas. *France at Bay, 1870–1871.* Barnsley, South Yorkshire, UK: Pen and Sword Military, 2011.

Feuillet, Mme. Octave. *Souvenirs et correspondances.* Paris: Calmann Lévy, 1896.

Gluckstein, Donny. *The Paris Commune: A Revolution in Democracy.* Chicago: Haymarket Books, 2011.

Gold, Arthur, and Robert Fizdale. *The Divine Sarah.* New York: Vintage Books, 1991.

Gottlieb, Robert. *Sarah.* New Haven: Yale University Press, 2010.

Haddon, Archibald. Green Room Gossip. London: Stanley Paul, 1922.

Hahn, Reynaldo. *La Grande Sarah: Souvenirs.* Paris: Hachette, 1929.

Hathorn, Ramon. "Sarah Bernhardt and the Bishops of Montreal and Quebec." *Historical Studies* 53 (1986): 97–120.

Horne, Alistair. *The Fall of Paris: The Siege and the Commune, 1870–71.* New York: St. Martin's Press, 1965.

Huret, Jules. Sarah Bernhardt. London: Chapman and Hall, 1899.

James, Henry. *The Portable Henry James.* New York: Penguin Books, 2004.

Johnson, Martin P. *The Dreyfus Affair: Honour and Politics in the* Belle Époque. Houndmills, Basingstoke, Hampshire, UK: Macmillan, 1999.

King, Ross. *The Judgment of Paris.* New York: Walker and Co., 2006.

Kobler, John. "Bernhardt in America." American Heritage, July/August 1989. (https://www.americanheritage.com/bernhardt-america; accessed May 22, 2019)

Labouchère, Henry Du Pré. Diary of the Besieged Resident in Paris. London: Hurst and Blackett, 1871.

La Fontaine, Jean de. *Fables from La Fontaine in English Verse.* London: John Murray, 1820.

"The Legend of Sarah Bernhardt." *Literary Digest*, February 28, 1914, 433–34.

"Madame Sarah Bernhardt—At Home in Sydney." *Sydney Mail and New South Wales Advertiser*, July 18, 1891, 127.

Marks, Patricia. *Sarah Bernhardt's First American Theatrical Tour, 1880–1881*. Jefferson, NC: McFarland and Co., 2003.

Martine, Paul. *Souvenirs d'un insurgé: la Commune 1871*. Paris: Librairie Académique Perrin, 1971.

McCullough, David. *The Greater Journey: Americans in Paris*. New York: Simon and Schuster, 2011.

"Mdlle. Sarah Bernhardt." *Victoria Magazine*. Vol. 30, *November 1877–April 1878*. London: Victoria Press, 1878.

Meltzer, Charles Henry. "Sarah Bernhardt as Her Friends Have Known Her." *Munsey's Magazine*, April 1917, 429–36.

Menefee, David W. *The First Female Stars: Women of the Silent Era*. Westport, CT: Praeger, 2004.

———. *Sarah Bernhardt in the Theatre of Films and Sound Recordings*. Jefferson, NC: McFarland and Co., 2003.

"Miscellanea." *Victoria Magazine*. Vol. 30, *November 1877–April 1878*. London: Victoria Press, 1878.

"A Modern Tragedy." *Outlook*, July 21, 1906, 640–41.

Morand, Eugène. *Les Cathédrales*. Paris: Librairie Théâtrale, Artistique et Littéraire, 1915.

Morse, John T., Jr. "The Dreyfus and Zola Trials." *Atlantic Monthly*, May 1898. (www.theatlantic.com/magazine/archive/1898/05/the-dreyfus-and-zola-trials/376186; accessed August 6, 2018)

Noël, Édouard, and Edmond Stoullig. *Les Annales du théâtre et de la musique*. Vol. 8, *1882*. Paris: Charpentier, 1883.

"Notes from Paris." *Truth*, April 13, 1882, 511–13.

"An Ode to Sara." *Chic*, November 3, 1880.

"Paris 1905–15." *Tate Online*. (www.tate.org.uk/whats-on/tate-modern/exhibition/century-city/century-city-paris-1905-15; accessed August 19, 2018)

Penesco, Anne. *Mounet-Sully: L'Homme aux cent cœurs d'homme*. Paris: Cerf, 2005.

Phillips, Stephen. *Panama, and Other Poems*. New York: John Lane Co., 1915.

Racine, Jean. *Britannicus*. London: George Bell and Sons, 1898.

Richardson, Joanna. *The Courtesans: The Demi-Monde in Nineteenth-Century France.* London: Weidenfeld and Nicolson, 1967.

———. *Sarah Bernhardt and Her World.* New York: Putnam, 1977.

Roberts, Mary Louise. *Disruptive Acts: The New Woman in Fin-de-Siècle France.* Chicago: University of Chicago Press, 2002.

Robins, Edward. *Twelve Great Actresses.* New York: G. P. Putnam's Sons, 1900.

Sand, George. *Agendas.* Vol. 4, *1867–1871.* Paris: Jean Touzot, 1993.

"Sarah Bernhardt." *Gouverneur Herald.* November 4, 1880, 2.

Sarcey, F. *Comédiens et comediennes.* Vol. 1, *La Comédie Française.* Paris: La Librairie des Bibliophiles, 1876.

Sarcey, Francisque. *Quarante ans de théâtre.* Paris: Bibliothèque des Annales politiques et littéraires, 1901.

Scribe, Eugène, and Ernest Legouvé. *Adrienne Lecouvreur.* New York: Darcie and Corbyn, 1855.

Skinner, Cornelia Otis. *Madame Sarah.* Boston: Houghton Mifflin, 1966.

Stoker, Bram. *Personal Reminiscences of Henry Irving.* London: William Heinemann, 1907.

Terry, Ellen. *The Story of My Life: Recollections and Reflections.* New York: McClure Co., 1908.

"To Sara B." *Chic,* October 20, 1880, 4.

"To Sarah Bernhardt." *The Palace Theater Presents Madame Sarah Bernhardt in Vaudeville.* New York: Martin Beck, 1912, unnumbered page.

West, Shearer. *The Image of the Actor.* New York: St. Martin's Press, 1991.

Zola, Émile. "J'Accuse . . . !" *L'Obs,* July 12, 2006. (nouvelobs.com/societe/20060712. OBS4922/j-accuse-par-emile-zola.html; accessed August 8, 2018)

Sarah Bernhardt: A Timeline

1844   Sarah Bernhardt is born in Paris. (October 22)

1851   Bernhardt is enrolled in boarding school.

1853   Transfers to Notre-Dame du Grandchamp,
a convent school in Versailles.

1860   Begins two years of study at the Conservatoire.

1862   Joins the Comédie-Française.

1863   Signs on with the Gymnase.

1864   Maurice Bernhardt is born. (December 22)

1866   Sarah Bernhardt is employed by the Odéon.

1869   Recognized for her work in *Le Passant*.

Appears in *Kean* and quiets a protest.

1870   Performs in *L'Autre*, under the direction of George Sand.

The Franco-Prussian War breaks out; Bernhardt
runs a hospital for wounded soldiers at the Odéon.

1872   Stars in *Ruy Blas* for the first time.

Returns to the Comédie-Française. (November 6)

1873   Notable roles include *Phèdre*.

Régine Bernhardt dies. (December 16)

1874   Sarah Bernhardt performs in *Zaïre*.

1876	The Paris Salon awards Bernhardt a silver medal for her sculpture *Après la tempête*.
	Performs in *Rome vaincue*.
	Youle Van Hard dies.
1878	Bernhardt rides in a hot-air balloon.
	Publishes *In the Clouds*.
1879	The Comédie-Française performs in London.
1880	Resigns from the Comédie-Française to form her own company of actors.
	Plays a dying courtesan in *La Dame aux camélias*, a foolish wife who comes to a tragic end in *Froufrou*, and an actor who was killed with poisoned flowers in *Adrienne Lecouvreur*.
	Embarks on her first American tour.
1881	Begins a six-month European tour.
1882	Stars in *Fédora*.
	Marries Ambroise Aristide (Jacques) Damala. (April 4)
	Appears on a Paris stage with Damala. (May 26)
1883	Bernhardt and Damala separate.
	Marie Colombier publishes *The Memoirs of Sarah Barnum*.
1884	Bernhardt scores a hit in *Théodora*.
1887	First performs in *La Tosca*.
1888	Moves to the boulevard Pereire.
	Maurice Bernhardt marries Maria Teresa (Terka) Jablonowska. (December 28)

1889   Granddaughter Simone Bernhardt is born.

        Jacques Damala dies. (August 18)

1890   Sarah Bernhardt portrays two historical figures, Cleopatra and Joan of Arc.

1891   Sarah Bernhardt leaves on a world tour.

1894   Purchases property on Belle-Île.

1895   Captain Alfred Dreyfus is stripped of his rank. (January 5)

1896   Granddaughter Lysiane Bernhardt is born.

        Sarah Bernhardt Day festivities honor the stage star. (December 9)

1898   A French newspaper publishes "*J'Accuse . . . !*"

1899   Bernhardt leases and renovates the theater that she calls the Théâtre Sarah Bernhardt.

        Takes on the leading role in *Hamlet*.

1900   Bernhardt launches another American tour.

        Madame Guérard and Jeanne Bernhardt die.

        Bernhardt makes her film debut with the duel from *Hamlet*.

        Stars onstage as Napoleon II in *L'Aiglon*.

1905   Bernhardt again begins an American tour.

        Saryta Bernhardt dies.

1907   Sarah Bernhardt publishes a memoir, *My Double Life*.

1908   Makes her final European tour.

1910   Once more visits America.

1910   Terka Bernhardt dies. (June)

1911   Lysiane moves in with Sarah Bernhardt.

Bernhardt stars in a film of *La Dame aux camélias*.

1912   Makes a film based on the life of Queen Elizabeth I of Great Britain.

1914   Receives the Legion of Honor. (March 6)

The assassination of Archduke Franz Ferdinand leads to the outbreak of World War I. (June 28)

Sarah Bernhardt and her family flee Paris. (September)

1915   Bernhardt's right leg is amputated above the knee. (February 22)

Bernhardt performs in *Les Cathédrales*. (November 6)

Entertains soldiers at the front.

Makes the film *Mères françaises*.

1916   Begins final American tour.

1918   Arrives in France; learns the war is over. (November 11)

1921   Last appearance in London, in the play *Daniel*.

Publishes a novel, *The Idol of Paris*.

1923   Acts in the film *La Voyante*.

The Art of the Theatre is published.

Sarah Bernhardt dies. (March 26)

Picture Credits

© Albert Harlingue/Roger-Viollet: 130, 149

Author's Collection: 8, 11, 16, 29, 31, 33, 40, 47, 51, 67, 70, 71, 73, 75, 76, 79, 82, 91, 95, 113, 115, 117, 119, 121, 151

Bibliothèque nationale de France: 137, 147, 156

Bibliothèque nationale, Paris, France, Archives Charmet/Bridgeman Images: 26

Billy Rose Theatre Division, the New York Public Library for the Performing Arts: 3, 4, 84, 153

© Charles Marville/Musée Carnavalet/Roger-Viollet: 80

The J. Paul Getty Museum: 6

© John Frost Newspapers/Mary Evans Picture Library: 135

Library of Congress: x, 19, 43, 44, 55, 61, 65, 66, 88, 93, 97, 111, 123, 125, 127, 128, 129, 132, 139, 141, 143, 144, 155, 178

Mary Evans Picture Library: 38

Mary Evans/SZ Photo/Scherl: 114

Print Collection, the New York Public Library: 21

Private Collection © Look and Learn/Bridgeman Images: 133

PVDE/Bridgeman Images: 100, 104

© Roger-Viollet: 57, 108

Tallandier/Bridgeman Images: 24

Yale University, Harvey Cushing/John Hay Whitney Medical Library: 59

During the Belle Époque, the Czech artist Alphonse Mucha created posters advertising Sarah Bernhardt's stage appearances.

Index